Combat Boots to Internet Millionaire

The 7-Figure Online Business Formula

Jason T. Miller

FIRST EDITION

ISBN: 978-1-957217-11-6 (paperback)
ISBN: 978-1-957217-12-3 (hardback)
ISBN: 978-1-957217-10-9 (ebook)

CONTENTS

Famous Quotes about Entrepreneurship

"Your work is going to fill a large part of your life, and the only way to be truly satisfied is to do what you believe is great work. And the only way to do great work is to love what you do."

– Steve Jobs, Co-founder CEO, Chairman Apple Inc.

"Don't limit yourself. Many people limit themselves to what they think they can do. You can go as far as your mind lets you. What you believe, remember, you can achieve."

– Mary Kay Ash, Founder Mary Kay Cosmetics

"Embrace what you don't know, especially in the beginning, because what you don't know can become your greatest asset. It ensures that you will absolutely be doing things different from everybody else."

– Sara Blakely, Founder SPANX

DEDICATION

This book is dedicated to all aspiring entrepreneurs that are, "Stepping Outside The Box" within their own lives, and was designed to help those that are willing to step outside their comfort zone and become the CEO of their own lives.

I would further like to dedicate this book to the military members and family members (my brothers and sisters) that have paid the ultimate sacrifice. The world is forever in your debt.

I wrote this book to bring forward new possibilities in your life as an entrepreneur. I want to give you the encouragement, tips, tricks and strategies I have used as an entrepreneur. I encourage you to think big and allow your creative imagination to skyrocket you to new heights in your life.

"There's lots of bad reasons to start a company. But there's only one good, legitimate reason, and I think you know what it is: it's to change the world."

– Phil Libin, CEO Evernote

Acknowledgement

I would like to personally thank my mentors that have helped me make this book possible and have influenced my decision-making process as an entrepreneur. I appreciate each of you and you know exactly who you are. Thank you for the valuable time, input and feedback that you have provided me as a business owner and entrepreneur.

Without your guidance, counsel and occasional tough love, our business would not be where it is today.

My family is forever in your debt and we appreciate you very much!

SPECIAL SHOUT OUTS

To my wife, Erika. I wouldn't be where I am without you. You are a very special woman, and I love you!

To my four wonderful children: Briana, Haylee, Barrett, and Vivian. I love all of you!

To my ultimate mentor and great friend T.J. Rohleder. You have been an inspiration and the best mentor one could ever ask for. Thank you for all of your mentorship and guidance.

To my family. All of you have influenced my life in one way or another, especially my father, Terry. Thank you for raising me tough and resilient and being there for me.

To every soldier that I have ever served with. "Those of you I respect, you know who you are! I salute you. Thank you for your service.

FOREWORD

A Few Simple Steps to Becoming a Millionaire

Becoming a millionaire isn't all that difficult and there are countless ways to achieve that milestone. Some people do it through real estate, others start their own business, while some simply get lucky by winning the lottery or winning big on a game show. What is even more interesting is that you don't have to be wealthy to begin with nor do you have to earn six figures to reach this goal.

I know some people who earn well over $100,000 per year and all they have to show for it is a large mortgage payment and a fancy car that depreciates faster than a glass of milk left outside in the summer sun. Anyone can become a millionaire and there are some things you need to do to have the best shot of making that a reality.

Earn Income

Clearly, the more money you make, the faster you can reach that milestone, but that doesn't mean your average Joe with an average income can't obtain millionaire status. The current median income in this country ranges between $35,000 - $60,000 dollars depending on where you live. Better yet, get married so you have dual incomes. The wonderful thing about having dual incomes is that even with two people in the household, your income may double, but your expenses typically don't.

If you don't earn even an average income, all is not lost. It is up to you to do something about it. A negative attitude about your job or your earning potential won't change anything. Be proactive and make the decision to improve your situation. It is your life, so take control and realize that things don't change overnight. It may take a few years of slow growth before you reach the point where you want to be, but you can do it if you really put your mind to it. Remember, short of inheriting money from a relative or winning the lottery, you will need reasonable income to become a millionaire.

Live Within Your Means

Ok, so you have income but now what? It doesn't matter how much money you make if you spend it all or spend even more than you make. It might be nice to eat out at nice restaurants every night, or to always be on the cutting edge of designer fashion but, this will only make you look like a millionaire to others instead of actually being a millionaire. This doesn't mean you have to live a miserable lifestyle, but you simply need to live reasonably. The bottom line is buying things and acting like a millionaire if you aren't will simply empty your bank account and give people a false impression of your status, but that's it.

Start by purchasing a home that you can comfortably afford and drive vehicles that suit your lifestyle without straining your budget. You don't have to be pulling down $75,000 a year and drive a 1992 Civic Hatchback or live in a dump, but throwing your money at a 4,000 square foot home in a gated community with luxury cars or SUVs that cost as much as one year of your salary won't help you become a millionaire. Some may argue that an expensive home and real estate in general is a good way to become a millionaire, but I will touch on that later.

Save Money

This isn't rocket science but if you earn a reasonable income and you live within your means, guess what, you will probably have money left over to save. But that's exactly the problem. Most people treat savings as an afterthought, or something that only gets attended to after all the other bills are paid. People pay bills, buy things, and then whatever is leftover they try to save. That is the wrong way to save.

I'm sure you've heard it before, but pay yourself first. Whether it is $100 a month or $1,000 a month, think of the savings as a bill that needs to be paid and do it regularly. If you are unable to save money you will find that your only wealth is in the form of material things. So, you need to start saving every month and you need to make it happen automatically. An online savings account can accomplish this for you, and on top of that you'll be earning better interest on that money than you would be at your local bank.

Invest Wisely

Now that you are saving money, you need to invest it wisely. Sticking it under the mattress or slowly building up in a savings account isn't going to help you reach your goals any faster. You don't have to read the Wall Street Journal or watch

CNBC everyday while actively managing your portfolio in order to be a good investor. Some of the best investment advice is to simply invest regularly and in a diversified portfolio. If you do this you'll already be doing more than most people and on your way to building wealth.

It is also important to remember that real estate is part of your investment picture, but it shouldn't be all of it. Too many people stake almost everything they have into a primary residence and expect it to appreciate in value. Just like any investment, generally speaking, over time you will make money. There isn't much debate about that, but relying heavily on real estate is no different than if you rely on one stock to fund your retirement. So, begin with opening up an investing account and put your money to work. It doesn't matter if you are investing in stocks, bonds, or index funds, but keeping costs down helps you keep more of your own money. There are many cheap places to start investing. Just do your homework and know what you are getting into!

You can become a millionaire by simply buying a single stock and holding onto it for 20 years. If it goes up significantly "You Win!" You can also buy a $500,000 home and have it double in value in 20 years, but these are pretty risky propositions. Take a lot of the risk out of the picture by making sure all of your eggs aren't in the same basket and develop an investment strategy that will provide steady growth over the years.

Start Your Own Business

Stepping outside of your comfort zone and investing in yourself and a business is an excellent way to become super wealthy. Like anything we do be it stocks or other investments, there are risks. Life is all about taking risk. If you're not a risk taker at some level than chances are you will never reach a wealthy or even rich lifestyle. You must be seeking that or you would not be reading this book!

Starting a business of your own and becoming your own CEO is very rewarding. About 15 years ago I started my first business and never looked back. Owning a business has allowed me to turn millions over and over again. There are pro's and con's to operating your own business but in my opinion the pro's more than outweigh the con's for sure.

Stick With Your Plan

Finally, if you have implemented some of the above strategies and are finding success than the only thing left to do is to continue doing it and stick to the plan. As far as income is concerned, always be on the lookout for ways to increase your income, whether it is through climbing the ladder at your current job, finding work elsewhere, or maybe even starting a business on the side. Increased income will mean you can save even more, provided you aren't foolishly spending the additional money. As that additional money gets tucked away into savings or investments it will continue to grow even more quickly.

It Isn't Hard to Do if You Work at It

Unfortunately, most people are looking for a way to get rich quick or to capitalize on the next big thing. It is true that some people have made their wealth through playing the real estate market, while others have done so by investing in a few stocks that exploded, but this is the exception and not the norm. If the above list seems overly simplistic, that's good. There are no secrets to becoming a millionaire and almost anyone has the chance to make it happen. The process is simple:

- Make money
- Don't spend all of your money
- Save some money
- Invest that money
- Possibly start a business
- Repeat

Certainly, there are many factors in play that can make this easier or more difficult for different people. This is simply the process that you can use in order to reach that goal, whether it is in 5 years or 50, if you follow a few basic steps you can do it. Take your dream and achieve it. Don't let people get you down and most of all invest in yourself to become the millionaire that you have always wanted to be.

Jason T. Miller
Jason T. Miller (U.S. Army, Retired)
Founder, Jump Start Marketing Concepts
Founder, Patriots to Business

CHAPTER 1

MY STORY AND HOW I GOT STARTED IN BUSINESS

My name is Jason Miller, and I grew up in a small town on the border of Montana and North Dakota. I grew up on a farm as a hard-working kid raising crops and tending livestock with my family.

We were a small farm operation that just made enough to live a comfortable life. My parents worked very hard to provide for my sister and I, but it was certainly a tough road and a lot of hard work for them. We were not poor by any means, but we fell in a common category like many, we lived comfortably.

There were certainly no luxury cars and fancy houses and certainly no beachfront property for a summer vacation home. But this taught me a valuable life lesson growing up.... Appreciate the things you do have.

My family has a long bloodline of military service and has served in many of the wars we have fought. Following a time-honored tradition, I joined the military at the ripe age of 17 and shipped off for basic training upon graduation from high school.

Upon completion of all my training as a new Infantryman I was assigned to my first duty station. I spent the first part of my career in a light Infantry Recon Platoon as a Scout Sniper and Spotter.

I have made many moves over the course of my 20+ year career in the military. I have seen many things and have been to many places both good and bad just like many of my fellow brothers and sisters at arms. Then my life changed. I met my beautiful wife Erika who was also in the military.

We instantly related being in the military and because of our common goals and desires for a future of personal, professional and financial independence. We moved from place to place as we all do in the military and realized that there has to be more.

After my wife got out of the military, she found it very difficult to start a career. She would just begin to climb the ladder of success just in time for us to make that next move to another duty station. So she did what many military spouses do and went to college. She now has two Masters Degrees, but has never fully been able to utilize her education because of moving every 3-4 years.

Like many, she has worked in jobs not careers. My wife and I have always had that sense that there was something better out there waiting for us. We have discussed many times the possibilities of starting our own business full-time and giving up the hectic life of the military. At the time I was well over the 10-year journey of my military career so it made sense to stick it out and get my 20 year retirement.

So fast-forward to 2014 - I deployed to Afghanistan and spent some time there assisting the Afghan Army rebuild and take control of their country. It was there that I had an absolute epiphany as I was sitting on my makeshift bed inside a sweatbox plywood room that was about the size of a prison cell. This is where the initial seeds were planted in my mind to take action and start our own online business. I knew I was quickly approaching retirement and needed to figure out a plan for our next chapter in life.

So there I was on the crappy make shift bed with crappy internet service searching for opportunities to make money with an online business. I did the research but ultimately set it aside as an idea upon redeployment home.

When I returned home and settled back into normal life, Erika and I began to reengage the discussion of starting our sustainable online business. I remembered the research I did on many business models when I was deployed, so we did more research and decided to give it a shot.

This was an opportunity for me to do when I retired and also an opportunity for my wife to have a meaningful career working from home. We decided to become an unstoppable team and start our own online business.

We wanted to create a lasting income that would allow us to spend more time together as a family and not have to live the normal 9-5 lifestyle dealing with traffic day-in and day-out and having to report to a "boss." We wanted to become the CEOs of our own lives by taking our years of military experience and pouring it into a solid business model.

Our goal has always been to earn a full-time income online and be the CEOs of our own lives. So we jumped in feet first and 100 miles an hour. We started attending business training, which was very relatable since training is second nature for us "military types." The training and business summits that we attended were easy to get through because it walked us through the initial process of setting up our online business step by step.

We reached out to industry leaders for mentorship to help walk us through the things we didn't fully understand.

The one thing that set us apart was our consistent drive to succeed at anything we do. The military has deeply instilled this attribute in both of us. This has served us well in our business ventures and has helped us reach new heights in our lives.

My wife and I will never have to work "normal" employee jobs ever again. Our military careers have been a driving factor in our success because of that sheer will to succeed. Like many, I enjoyed the last 20+ years of my military career. It has been exciting, rewarding and has taken care of my family in many ways that the outside world cannot relate to.

However, we have now found a new start and a new journey down another path in our lives as successful entrepreneurs helping others find their success in life.

Now, to be honest business up to this point was not completely new. In 2001 I started my first eBay business online. I nurtured this business for almost 14 years and it was also very successful. Running a multiple six figure eBay business is not an easy task. Imagine shipping thousands of items from your home without a central storage and shipping facility!

eBay was a fun and exciting business but it grew out of control. I often tell people we got too big for our britches in the physical products niche. Then we found the power of digital products and the ability to license products as affiliate marketers.

This really changed the game and is how we have been able to build a sustainable online business today. Coupled with our own digital learning products of our own, we can license other company's products and sell them for a cut of the final cost of the sale.

Now that we are established in the industry, we have been able to create multiple six figure quarterly sales in our business through cultivating multiple income streams. In this book I will show you some of my best tips and tricks to help you do the very same thing! Read every page of this book and feel free to reach out to us on our website anytime!

CHAPTER 2

FILTHY RICH –
THINK LIKE THE WEALTHY

Being wealthy does not have to be difficult if you have the know-how. In these hard economic times many people are satisfied by just getting by and scraping enough money together to pay the bills.

Wealth and financial freedom are a far-off dream for many people. For them, it means mansions, gated communities, a fast car, private parties or a pool. The truly wealthy have family names like Rockefeller or Morgan.

It can be easy to accumulate wealth. The thing is, not everyone knows how. The twentieth century has brought a boom of first-time millionaires, many of which do not come from family money. They make their first million by employing timeless wealth wisdom and secrets only the ultra-rich used to know. Fortunately for you, there are dozens, even hundreds of little wealth nuggets you can easily apply to your life to expand your portfolio and double, even triple your net worth.

Being smart with money and becoming wealthy is not rocket science, but for many it looks and feels like hard work. The fact of its very simplicity means that more and more people should know and be doing this. But they are not. This is because most people do not know how to make money work for them, not the other way around. This is also because making money involves patience and restraint. Everything about our culture advocates otherwise.

But do you want to end up broke by the time you retire? Do you constantly fend off phone calls from creditors? Do you sigh and shake your head at your bank balance? No one wants to spend their life waiting for payday and watching money flutter away the moment bills come in the mail.

Becoming wealthy is not just about falling into family money, inheriting a trust fund or even having a big income. In fact, many people with huge incomes rarely are truly wealthy. Huge incomes often equal huge expenses and struggling to keep your finances in the black every month does not equal financial freedom. Investing is different from spending. Someone who has a huge house or houses and a great car may look rich but may not be.

Affluence and wealth can be hard to come by. If you are looking for secrets to getting millions or simply looking for a way to manage your money, this is it. This book will teach you the secrets of the truly wealthy and is a step-by-step guide on how to get there. You will learn everything from gaining financial freedom to basic investing and secret tips from business giants all over the world.

True financial freedom is only a step away, if you know how. Are you ready to start becoming truly wealthy? These gems and secrets are designed to help you turn your resources, whatever they may be, into true wealth. This Chapter can help you whether you follow it step by step or choose a few tactics to start with.

Creating a wealth foundation:
Earning financial freedom

Creating the wealth mindset: The wealthy think differently. This is true and an inescapable fact. The other thing is that there is a poor mindset and a wealthy one.

The rich have a different approach to life. They plan, risk and manage their money in a different manner. They also have a positive attitude towards life and opportunities. The first and most important step to true financial freedom is creating this mindset for yourself. This also involves a no-holds barred, honest look at your life and assets.

Creating a starting place is as important as moving forward, so it does not matter if you start with $1 or $1,000,000. It is all about the mindset and the will to move forward to creating your wealth.

Redefine what wealth means for you. Being "rich" simply is a term for many people. Technically, wealth or being wealthy is defined as having an abundance of resources or possessions. The high life does not equal wealth. Having a gigantic mortgage for a beautiful home or a huge car payment does not equal wealth.

Are status symbols your end goal? Does wealth for you mean that ability not to worry about bills or how much is left in your checking account at the end of the month? Does it mean providing comfortably for your family or being free from financial worry? Does it mean the ability to afford luxury designer goods or getting a membership to the local country club? Being rich or being wealthy can also mean you enjoy a comfortable retirement.

Does wealth mean something totally different to you? Your definition of wealth goes a long way towards setting your goals.

Another important step when it comes to managing your wealth is to set goals. Start with an overall battle plan, such as "By the end of the year, I will have at least $500,000 in savings." Why? You need to be a visionary to be wealthy. A common factor that sets the millionaire apart from the average Joe is this: they know they wanted to be wealthy and they were willing to take the steps to reach their goal.

To reach one goal, you have to make smaller goals and reach them. Every little step you take, every penny you save matters. Use smaller goals as stepping stones. For example, to save that $500,000, one needs to set aside $50,000 every single month, invest or cut down expenses.

Manifest your financial destiny by setting your subconscious towards specific goals. Create dream charts by cutting out pictures of your dream status or words that empower to help fuel your subconscious and get you to wear you want to go. Never underestimate the power of your will and mind. Wealthy people never say they cannot do it, they think of ways so that they can. Write it down. Seeing what you want, and getting what you want involve seeing it in black and white.

Know how much you are worth. Take stock of all your assets and income and subtract your debt. Many people go through life financially blind, not knowing how much they are worth or how much they owe and often end up blindsided by money.

The test: Your age x (your average household income from all sources – inheritance) divided by 10 = your net worth. The rich have a net worth often double or triple the amount. The average American has less than half. The goal is to double your net worth.

The truly wealthy consider themselves as the foremost asset. Accordingly, they pay themselves first. They also tend to invest in themselves first, especially when it comes to education. Take classes and groom yourself to be the millionaire, entrepreneur and success you want to be.

Guard your ideas with the passion of the Secret Service. Commodities are now no longer limited to labor, but have expanded to include ideas, imagination and opportunities.

Keep in mind that the average millionaire is not who you think he is. The frugal rich stay richer—if you do not believe this, think of all those high flying celebrities who end up with their homes in foreclosure or selling their tell-all's on TV to pay for all that Cristal and all those houses.

The famous IKEA owner drives a Volvo. HSBC's chairperson famously goes around the main office turning off all the lights long after the employees have left. The stories go on and on. The rich do not live the lifestyle of the rich—they stay rich because they are frugal misers at heart.

Assess your income and what you can do with it. 80% of modern millionaires were able to get there on annual incomes of $55,000 or less. Even meager savings eventually add up to thousands or millions of dollars.

When you look at a job, always know how much the head honcho gets paid because this will later affect your income in terms of promotion, benefits and future potential earnings. If you are gunning for a six figure salary and the current CEO is getting by on $300,000 a year, then maybe the job is not for you.

Find alternative ways to generate income if you are unhappy about your current level of earnings or the amount of the salary you currently have. This can mean looking for other employment with better pay or benefits or finding ways to boost your income little by little. This can mean starting a cottage industry business, learning to invest, buying and selling online or any number of means to add to your nest egg.

Create forms of passive income, the type of income that you receive with little to no effort. Examples of this include: rent from property you own, licensing patents or dividends and returns from investments.

Passive income can come from many sources. Exploiting the business possibilities of the Internet through blogs or sales from eBay or Amazon is one way to add to your income with minimal effort. The truly wealthy prefer passive income anytime. It frees up time for you to do what you want, even while you earn.

Be diverse. Create streams of income, do not rely on one large river. A job that pays $3M is great, but an accident or sudden layoff can cut you off. Think outside your salary. A job paying you $1M a year, plus real estate profits that amount to $1M and another $1M from stock is a far easier and safer thing to manage.

Learn to hold off gratification. A wealthy person knows how to delay gratification and sacrifice the now for later. This often comes with a positive attitude towards work and wealth, such as: "If I invest now, I will make 10% more later." The wealthy do not think of now, they think of the future. The present is merely an opportunity.

Change your mentality about spending. Do you really have to have that (fancy car) now? The truly rich hold off gratification, knowing that what is trendy, popular or a must have today may not last until tomorrow. Never be frightened of failure.

Be realistic. Growth and wealth do not appear overnight, unless you are lucky enough to win the lottery or find long lost treasure.

Investments need time to mature and savings need time to accumulate. Patience will be well rewarded. The wealthy know that scrimping now will lead to better results in the future.

Create a sense of urgency in your life. Do not wait for things to happen to you. You may think that you are playing safe by waiting around or looking for the next big deal. This is the financial equivalent of sitting around. Take risks, invest, start the business now.

Seize opportunities the moment they happen. The first to get there often wins, leaving the losers in the dust.

Taking stock of what you have right now can have some advantageous surprises. For one, you may find out that you have more than you think. Second, it gives you a clear cut place to start and helps you find balance as well as set goals. After all, you cannot move forward without knowing where you come from.

Cutting corners where they matter

When it comes to wealth generation, another important factor that is hard to follow is "living within your means." For many people, living in debt has become the norm. It is common for the average person to be buried in debt before they reach the age of 25. A consumer-driven economy based on floating credit also creates the impression that wealth means more products. After taking a hard look at your assets and income, now you have to check your lifestyle and see where you can cut down on expenses.

Write down your expenses. Do not lie to yourself. There is nothing like seeing it in black and white (or red). Keep track of your expenses on a spreadsheet or if you prefer, in a notebook. It gives you a concrete idea of where you are spending too much and where you are spending too little.

If you are looking to save more, write down everything you buy and keep track of it. Do you really need to spend $5 a day on designer coffee? That amounts to $1800 dollars a year just on your morning cup of Joe. Is it paramount to have the latest car every single year when you are hip deep in auto loans?

Cut those credit cards. The average person owns at least seven cards. The average number you need to sustain a good to great credit score? The answer is one or two. One well-managed card does more for your credit score than the dozen overextended cards you have. If you can manage without one, why not cut them all? Your credit score is not just affected by cards, but by other loans you have in your name, like your mortgage or auto loan.

Ruthlessly cut out all the services you do not need and monitor those you do. One millionaire famously counted the sheets in toilet paper rolls because he thought suppliers were overcharging him. He was right.

Before you cut those cards, however, understand the utilization ratio: the total credit used versus the total credit available to you. Many people keep multiple cards for fear that one or more lines will be cut, increasing the ratio over time. The goal is to have a very low ratio compared to debt, low balances and even lower interest.

Get a free copy of your credit report. Dispute any outdated items. Keep in mind that items should slide off, not stay on. Focus on judgments, liens and any items that undermine your potential to lenders.

Understand how interest affects your debt. The wealthy understand how interest works for investments, for loans and how it compounds over time. Those who are not wealthy do not.

Compound interest is interest that is added to the principle at certain intervals on the debt. This means that the loan/balance of a certain loan gets higher over time and you end up paying more interest.

Compounding rates differ but can be legally done on a yearly, quarterly, yearly or even daily basis. A loan with a starting principal of $1000 charged with 20% interest per year turns into $1200 at the end of the first year and so on. In contrast, simple interest does not add to the principal of the loan, but is the amount charged for use of that money or loan.

PAY DEBT OFF ASAP. Pay more than the minimum on loans.

Satisfy the interest and part of the principal—the debt amount will lessen over time and the bonus is you pay it off faster. The more you pay now, the less you pay later. Keep records of any and all transactions over the Internet or phone, especially if you are fixing your finances.

Print or save any changes to your account. When calling customer service, ask for the representative's employee number and record the time of the call in the event you need to follow up on a request. Keep exact files and amounts. Keep copies of everything.

Be hyper-vigilant when it comes to cards, loans or mortgages. Look for ways to lower interest, increase payments and keep an eye out for changes that could affect your loans.

Make a budget and stick to it. Think of it as a budge-it. Once you make it, you do not budge-it. Monthly and weekly budgets should be calculated to the penny.

The truly wealthy or those who want to be consider debt to be death to their portfolio. They only allow themselves to go into debt when they need it, and in that case they often refer to it as capital or even better, they often get it from someone else.

Keep the motto in mind when working with debt and get rid of it as soon as possible. Separate your accounts to keep track of your money. Keep a savings account, an investment account and an earnings account.

Know the consequences of forbearing or deferring loans. The breathing room you get is often paid back threefold in capitalized interest or an increased loan principal.

Create an emergency fund or funds. These accounts should contain the equivalent of 3 to 6 months' salary using low risk accounts (savings, certificates of deposits or insured money market accounts) as a safety net not just for your finances but for unexpected events in your life. This prevents you from dipping into your earnings or cashing in other income resources when unexpected and unwanted events happen, such as sudden illness.

Remember that you can grow rich now on money that you are throwing away. To be truly wealthy, you have to know that a simple dollar is an investment goldmine.

On average, millionaires spend more time selecting what to buy than buying the product itself. Why? Because they look for the best bargain before laying their money down—and ask for discounts before making a selection. Apply this principal to your life and watch your expenses go down.

Instead of selecting the first brand-name product you see, take the time to check what exactly you are getting. For example, many commercially branded cereal and grain products have exactly the same nutritional content as their generic cousins, at almost twice the price. Remember that you are paying more for the brand than you are for the product itself.

Millionaires and the wealthy also know the value of patience. Many stay in the first home they bought long after they can afford a more expensive one. Never accept a deal at face value. Negotiate until you feel the terms are in your favor.

The most important thing you should know is that without financial freedom, you cannot be truly wealthy. The most important thing is to create a base: a lower debt to income ratio and leeway to save and put money aside for investing later on.

It also frees up your mind so you can implement the law of attraction. Implementing positive thinking in your life can draw in positive forces and create more and more goodwill and luck. It is hard to think positive when you are constantly worrying about bills or making payments. By thinking positive and creating more positivity in your life, you bring in not just monetary wealth but a wealth in your personal life as well.

Investing and managing your wealth: Becoming truly wealthy

Once you have established a firm financial foundation or put aside a little money, it is time to learn to invest. Many first-time investors fall into the trap of waiting, and waiting until they "have enough." The first thing you have to do is nix that notion, right now. You will find out by reading the tips that even measly amounts can add up to great amounts over time.

Others balk at investing because they think "I do not know enough to be a player." That is right. You do not. The truly wealthy understand how money works and never start sentences with the words "I do not know." If you do not understand investing and how it works, it is time to start to do the legwork.

Investing 101

The primary focus of investing is making your money work for you instead of working for your money. Many wealthy people have perfected the art of creating their wealth instead of giving a service. Building wealth also means creating wealth that is sustainable and continues to generate even in the event that you are unable to work.

Learn the difference between having a high income and being truly wealthy. High incomes do not necessarily mean that you are rich, especially if this income comes from only one source.

The myth persists that you can only be truly wealthy if you come into family money or are born into a home of silver spoons, silk sheets and antique furniture. Continue to believe in this myth, and you still have the mindset of the poor.

Many of the middle class believe that a high-income job is the end all of their existence and work their butts off to get to a position that pays in five or six digits but end up baffled at how little they have by the time retirement rolls around.

For example, the average high-level manager earns $200,000 a year, with benefits but stands to lose that income in the event of layoffs or illness. Although his income earning potential is high, it only comes from one source.

Contrast that with a middle level manager earning $50,000 a year. This middle manager, however, rents out properties in the city for another $500,000 and reaps dividends from stocks and bonds for another $100,000 a year. In the event of illness, death or mass layoffs, half of his earning potential is still secure.

The source of the latter's income is also easily passed on to future generations, securing wealth for the middle level manager's family.

Choose your investment goals as these will decide your allocation strategy later on. A broker or brokerage firm can help you decide on what your plans are, as well as help you begin investing.

Research the different types of investments as well as how risky they are. In general:

Stocks – you purchase partial ownership of a company and as part- owner, are entitled to annual profits. However, many people buy stock to sell when the price is high, not for dividends. The practice of buying low and selling high is relatively low risk but the potential for reward is governed by market and highly emotional changes. Yes, stock is considered an emotional asset.

Bonds – bonds are small loans to companies or governments that the investor pays for. They usually have fixed interest rates and are considered very safe and low risk investments. T-bills, municipal bonds and corporate bonds are some examples.

Mutual fund – this involves pooling money together with other like- minded investors to buy a full portfolio, usually run by firms or money managers. This type of investment is often the starting point for many first-time investors, simply because it provides a more diverse portfolio from the get-go.

REITS – these are companies that deal primarily with the ownership of real estate and manage a portfolio for you. They have the advantage of being diverse and easy to sell—as well as reduce the headache of managing your own property.

Other alternatives – Generally these are the high-risk and high reward securities where the payoff can be huge, but the risk is high. Real estate, commodities, FOREX, options and futures fall under this category.

Create an allocation strategy for your savings or income to minimize risk and spread out your investments to guarantee several streams of income versus just one.

Learn about investing and accounting before you start spreading the money around. Consult with brokers or brokerage firm, especially if you have a lot to invest. Take night courses or read investment books to understand what you are getting into.

For example, you have $100,000 dollars to invest. 35% ($35,000) could go to property or real estate, another 30% for stocks, 10% for venture capital, etc. An allocation strategy helps you maximize your investments and also gives you the ability to indulge in some high- risk behavior, if you so wish, without losing all your capital. The financial equivalent of putting all your eggs in one basket, such as investing in all one type of equity, is portfolio suicide.

Account for every cent, every nickel, every dime and quarter. The saying goes you never know the value of money until you have to dig around the couch cushions for it. The truly wealthy know that every penny can be put to good use. Money is stagnant only when you want it to be, or when it flies out of your hands.

Even small amounts matter. Many people say they will invest only when they have x amount, but even a small investment of $1000 can give you great returns in the future. By thinking of returns instead of instant cash or how much you have on hand, you create your wealth through possibilities.

Saving 10,000 a year with a 10% rate of return and seeding that account with an additional 10,000 per year will yield $128,000+ after 10 years. If you start with $5,000, you end up with about $94,000 after said 10 years. That doesn't count the interest the account would generate for years after.

Invest your money as early as you can. The true friend of money is always time and the passage of it. The longer money sits and the more interest it collects, the higher the chances that you will reap thousands of dollars in returns.

A great example for this is the 401(k). Many Americans simply cannot wait until retirement and cash it in as soon as they can. But for what? A faster car, a bigger house or in some cases, that giant flat screen TV everyone else has.

Your 401(k) alone is a savings plan you must NEVER touch. Do the math. If you have an annual salary of $100,000 and contribute 10%, with a 50% employer match rate and no salary increases, you end up with $ 741,184.02 in 20 years. Increase the contribution to 12%, with all other factors constant and the amount rises to $889,420.89. Increase the time frame to 30 years and you end up with $2 million.

Buy stock, not product. If you love the product, chances are others will to. So why waste time buying the product when you can make money off the stock. This creates:

a) Passive income and

b) A higher chance of return on investments.

Take Apple. Apple's stock has risen over 12 times in the past five years, quadrupling dividends for investors. How many iPhones or iPods have you bought over the past five years? How much money do you think an average shareholder has made from the products you have been buying? Even with the death of its founder, Steve Jobs, Apple's stock remained strong and rose. Traditionally company stock falls with the death of visible CEOs or front men, but this was not true in this case.

One exception: keep in mind that sales do not make the stock. Activision is a company that markets and makes one of the biggest selling video games in the world, with sales totaling over 400,000 on the first day of the new installment release. However, their stock and shares have remained static for around 4 years.

Create assets that will make money for you with a minimum of effort. For example, investing in a restaurant does not require you to show up daily to manage the day-to-day running of the business, only to pay the management firm or keep the standard of a franchise.

Think long term. The truly wealthy do not count on single projects that net huge paychecks, but invest in opportunities that create returns and dividends that last for years. Long term also means the ability of securities to mature. Thinking long term means having the ability to see the future in a sense—and finding projects that affect and create these futures.

Do not wait for business opportunities, create them. Entrepreneurs look at an empty lot and see possibility and a method for them to get rich. Those with a poor mindset simply see an empty lot. The rich look at garbage and see a garbage hauling business, a rust- cleaning service, a recycling center. Those with a poor mindset see only the discarded tires, the dirt and the weeds.

Another great secret is to never care where you money comes from. Many people balk at investing in businesses that are not "sexy" perhaps because they do not want to tell people at parties that they got rich off sewage.

Truly wealthy people spread their money around and reap them in regardless if they were earned because of sewage or flowers. Who cares if it comes up in cocktail conversation?

Always think in terms of specific assets versus their overall value in the market. The truly wealthy do not rely on the ups and downs of the market, but the possible opportunities that stem from them.

For example, the real estate market may be down during the recession but right now savvy investors are buying up foreclosed property in great locations for half prices for later investment.

Know when to hold off, reassess and quit. Investors will say no. But not all of them will. Those with a poor mindset go to the bank for a loan, get rejected and never think about their idea or opportunity again. The wealthy mindset goes to the bank for a loan, gets rejected, and redrafts the proposal and returns to get the approval.

The poor mindset goes into business not knowing the risks of the deal and is baffled when the fallout occurs. The wealthy mindset goes into a deal, knows the risk and gets out if things are going bad. Always follow your gut and do your research. Knowing when to back off from risky or unethical deals will not only save your money but have effects on your financial freedom.

Accept that there will be instances where you will experience some loss, such as when stock goes down or remains stagnant, therefore not providing you with the expected dividends. Accept that this will change as well.

Do not join the bandwagon: just because everyone is putting their money in it, does not mean you should. Get rich quick schemes are simply schemes.

Forget compartmentalizing your money. Every penny is important so do not think of it as a bonus or extra pay. The wealthy put every single cent to good use and are able to account for all of them.

The lesson here is to value every single dollar you earn. One millionaire started by investing $25, that is right, $25 in a mutual fund. He could not afford any more at the time, since he worked a menial job. As his pool grew, so did the amount of his investments. He is now worth multi-millions.

Learn about taxes and how to use them to your advantage, not the other way around.

The truly wealthy know how to make taxes work for them. Never be afraid to learn and ask. Instead of having someone do it for you, learn how to do it yourself.

Finally, never invest if you are not willing to wait. Otherwise, you are throwing your money away like a gambling addict at a poker table.

The truly wealth think of investing as a game that pays out and is fun to play. Never for once think that they got there by simple luck. It takes a lot of research, studying and waiting to get there. The poor make excuses and say, they never have enough time between their jobs, their family and whatever other obligations they have.

The wealthy create the time to invest and invest in their time as well. However, the main difference is this: they enjoy it. They enjoy the time they spend reading investment books. They enjoy reading the reports, watching the stock market and simply love the game of money. This is an attitude you need to become successful when you move to invest. This is the attitude that makes winners and makes the wealthy.

Making and protecting your money

The average millionaire or comfortably wealthy person works for himself or owns a business. This is a law that is hard to follow. Most people think a business is a risky proposition simply because there are so many factors that affect the success of a business. A million things can go wrong, but a million things can also go right.

The wealth mindset is one that works for itself, cashing in on your own ideas and labor. The poor mindset works for others, laboring for a minimum cut of the profit.

The idea of working for yourself can be scary. Many first-time business owners fail because they sink everything they have into one venture and never recommit when the road to success gets rocky. The wealthy and the rich stick with their business plan and move forward regardless of the events, and are confident in their success.

Do something that you love, because you will never feel like it is work. The success stories of many entrepreneurs and millionaires always begin with this line "I love...[insert hobby, passion or interest here] so I "

Money always follows passion and the upside is, you will never feel like you worked a day in your life. Ask yourself what you love to do, what you are good at and how important it is to you. Once you know what it is, you will know what venture to begin.

Alternatively, find a need for something you love and fill it. Filling a need or creating a need is an excellent starting point for a business. Curves Gym combined the owner's need for fitness and hatred of being ogled while at the gym.

She provided a women's only gym without mirrors, filling a need many women did not even know existed. Women lined up around the street to work out at this gym and it boasts hundreds of franchises around the US today.

Do not be afraid to do something humble—many a business has expanded from humble origins and cottage industries. No idea is too small, no business is "stupid".

Make sure your business fits your lifestyle. If you hate nightclubs, why start one? Why start a golfing business when you have never picked up a club in your life and have no interest in doing so?

Those who cannot run a business, invest in one. It takes the headache out of the management and gives you profit without the effort.

The wealthy know when to expand their business. Those who want to be truly rich run multiple businesses. Take Nigella Lawson, who started with a cooking show and now has a line of products and even utensils. One business, different umbrellas. Different umbrellas, one profit.

The business should never be static, but it should be familiar. Take a cue from top restaurants. They constantly change or update their menus but keep the customer favorites around.

Be the best. There are no exceptions to this rule. Provide the best service, the fastest delivery, the highest quality, and the newest products. Follow these rules and the customers will come.

A sub rule to this secret is to always strive to continue to be the best. Once you have set a standard, customers and clients will expect you to maintain it. Many a business has experienced fallout after reaching heights due to declining service or worsening product. Take a cue from timeless products and services that continue to make money over the years.

They never balk or shirk when it comes to quality. Even if it means making their customers pay a little extra.

Your business is defined by its employees—especially if you decide to go into any type of service industry. Hire for attitude, train for skill. Never keep an employee who is not worth the salary you pay.

Never tolerate stupidity, slowness or excuses. Instead, screen, evaluate and expect change. Millionaires never take slack from their employees. They never hesitate when the time comes to let one go.

Learn to recommit. Every business owner experiences fall out, bad sales or some sort of failure. There will always be a time when you fall into the red. It takes perseverance to go back into the black.

Economize where it counts. Find the best deals for raw product to maximize profit.

The truly wealthy know how to make profit with minimal expenditure. Reduce overhead, especially when it comes to trappings. A huge corner office with the antique desk and leather seats will not mean much when you are scrambling to pay the bills.

Protecting your money

Once you have money, you will take time to protect it by avoiding future catastrophes. Be cautious and always assume the worst. Do not go through life thinking that other people will not take advantage of you or that your money is not important to them. A careless mistake can cost you a fortune. A careless demeanor opens you up to attack. And you will never know where it is going to come from.

Now that you have the money, you have to take the steps to protect it from unscrupulous beings. Many a millionaire's downfall came from lawsuits from hungry money-grubbing relatives or the greed from immediate family. The media is packed with celebrity stories where the 'evil' spouse gets millions in the divorce, millions they never earned simply because the high earner took no precautions.

In the case of lawsuits, anything personal amounts to what you or your companies are worth. Lawyers love public information and can easily figure out what you are worth by accessing public records. Transferring the bulk of your wealth to foundations, trusts or corporations ensures that these stay well out of the public's eye or are untouchable in the event you are attacked.

Protecting your money now ensures that it will continue to benefit you and your family for years and decades to come.

Millionaires and the truly wealthy never put assets in their name and guard their personal assets zealously. They use corporations and protect themselves with liability insurance. Corporate entities are used to operate businesses, partnerships are made with the idea that if all goes to hell, it is time to get out. Use trusts, family partnerships and protect your personal assets and wealth.

Turn yourself into a stealthy, moving target. Never be conspicuous about your wealth and forego the trappings of it. Remember: the bigger, flashier bird is always easier to bring down. The birds that fly low, fly below the radar and detection.

Begin asset protection early to prevent any mishaps. Never let yourself get caught in the trap of beginning asset protection when you are already in heaps of trouble!

There is nothing like being prepared. Besides, transferring assets when you are being sued is illegal and can land you in jail (plus you lose everything). Protect your personal assets from claims and unscrupulous parties!

Create a clear-cut and legal will, even if you are only 32 years old. Make sure you know where your money is going. Many people put off the idea of the will simply because it makes them face their own mortality which is always wrong.

Update and notarize yearly, or anytime you like. A will prevents many a family feud, protects your interests long after you are gone and ensures that money that you share keeps going where you want it to go. Without a will, chaos will ensue, especially if your personal fortune and business assets are worth six digits or more.

For businesses, the equivalent of a will is known as succession planning. Many successful businesses have failed because an epic predecessor was not able to carefully plan who would succeed him in the event of his death.

Follow the example of Steve Jobs and create a succession plan for your business *before you even get sick or retire*. Many family corporations create a version of this by grooming successors from within the family and stipulating conditions to be met in order to inherit or run the business.

Never enter any partnership, including conjugal ones, without a back-up plan or a clear way out. That is what prenuptial agreements are for. Do not let a future ex-spouse pull a Paul McCartney on you.

Never put all your money into one humungous deal. Diversity is the key to true wealth. Keep in mind that those eggs in one basket are more liable to break if the basket is too heavy.

The final timeless wealth secret. Money is meant to shared, not hoarded. Follow the Rockefeller rule: 10% of your worth is meant to be shared. This creates more for you.

Conclusion

There is no shortcut to instant wealth. Being rich means playing a game that lasts for years. The truly wealthy not only look forward to this game, but also look forward to playing it. By following these timeless secrets, you learn the value of hard work, patience and reap the rewards for years to come.

Never be complacent and put off your wealth creation for tomorrow. True wealth and real wealth starts by making these changes today. Break that piggy bank and start investing *now*.

Wealth creation is both a complex strategy and a waiting game, but by following these tips, you can be on your way to true wealth, a comfortable lifestyle and living your life financially free.

CHAPTER 3

ULTIMATE TRAFFIC PART I - PROSPECT TO CUSTOMER

P eople are creatures of habit, and that knowledge can be used to convert visitors into customers. If you pay close attention to when people are triggered to open their wallets, then you can use the same dynamics to develop a strategy to have it work for your sales efforts. Understanding triggers that produce sales is one effective way to develop strategies that can work over a large cross-section of people.

In each part of this chapter, we will discuss a variety of different techniques to mine your traffic for sales, explaining what works, the psychological impact of the strategy, and even the how to implement for the best timing and results. The first strategy we will discuss exploits people's tendencies to develop habits and uses that to create sales that get bigger and bigger as they become more involved with you.

The strategic plan

For a habit to work for you, it has to produce the close of a sales call to action. For instance, if you've ever been to the deli, you'll see how this strategy works to make additional sales.

You go and you order 1/2 lb. of lunch meat, it doesn't matter which. Odds are, that they will cut up more than you need, never less, and then when they weigh it they'll ask: "Is that okay or do you want me to take off some?" Since you already committed to the order of 1/2 lb. of lunch meat, you'll seem cheap trying to get out of the extra so most of the time you let it go and pay for the extra. Not only that, but when they hand you the lunch meat they ask: "Is there anything else I can get for you?" And, since you've already purchased one item, you are more inclined to purchase another.

This strategy works because you already committed to a purchase, no matter how small, and asking for something on top is taking advantage of the groove you've already slipped into. It may not seem like a lot of extra money going in your pocket, but if you do this to every single sales prospect you encounter, the multiple effect can line your pockets quite nicely.

This strategy works okay with retail sales, but it is dynamite with direct sales on the Internet. The key is to get your visitor to commit to a small sale first and then before they check out, ask them if they want something extra. You will be surprised how fast your orders tend to grow after that.

The psychological triggers

The biggest resistance people tend to have when closing a sale is just the simple act of saying "yes." Once that obstacle is circumvented it becomes much easier to make the sales larger out of pure inertia. Once people are already walking in a specific direction it takes more effort and attention to change directions than it does to just keep going the way you're already headed.

Some people like to call it consistency in action, but it's also about habitual action. Psychologists say that it only takes so much time to create a habit, but it can take more than 21 days to break it and it takes a concerted effort to do so. People generally don't pay attention to their habits and that's why when you identify a trigger it is easy to exploit it to your benefit.

You are actually setting the course without making it obvious to your sales prospect. The minute they agree to even a tiny purchase, you have set the momentum to generate even larger sales, if not immediately – at least, down the road.

How to implement effectively

The trick here is to make the first purchase as simple and as easy as possible. It doesn't even have to be a major purchase. You aren't trying to score a huge sale, you are trying to involve your sales prospect in your business at this point. There's plenty of time to expand their sales later. So, make that first sale as easy and as painless as possible.

This works beautifully online by having a very simple and cheap offer on your home page. It can be anything really, as long as it is a simple process and can produce an immediate effect. Reports and media downloads make very good initial sales online because you can sell them cheap, in mass quantities, and you can also deliver it electronically for an immediate effect. You have a check box to put them on an email or newsletter list too to help you capture their email and allow you to market them for more products later.

With a little research, you can find out what products your customers bought after they bought your initial lead sales package. Then, you can target new customers with that as it's already proven to be a winner. This can lead to larger sales down the road.

However, if you want to implement this strategy immediately, it takes a little more finesse. In the retail, face-to-face world, you would simply do like the deli clerks and offer another product to add to someone's check-out. New home construction companies do this all the time, by calling them "upgrades." You sign for a basic unit and then they start asking you if you want to upgrade the countertops with marble, put in hardwood floors instead of carpet, and so on.

Pretty soon, the price you committed to buying comes out to an exorbitant amount with all the additional things you've consented to buy. And, should you decide you don't have enough money for everything you want, you're stuck with the difficult decision to figure out what you can cut out of your home package. Obviously, the answer is that it's just too difficult to decide what features or options you don't want, instead it's much easier to charge it.

That's why stores also make their payment options as simple and easy as possible. The more payment options you have, the easier it is to close a sale and overrule any objection on a lack of money. Some stores even ante up the ease of purchase by offering their own in- house financing. These financing offers usually start fairly low and come with very little risk on the part of the store, but it can't help to convert sales prospects into bonafide customers.

At any rate, to implement this at the end of a small sale, all you simply have to do is ask, almost as an afterthought, "Oh! Do you want to include this x offer too?" It can be very effective if you are doing this face-to-face and you've already got up to leave and just before departing suddenly realize you forgot to tell them about that extra offer that would go good with his sale.

The key is to be subtle; the hard sell online only makes people mad if you sign them up for extra offers in sneaky, underhanded ways. Always get the customer's approval clearly before charging them for the sale. This can be done at checkout by simply adding an extra page they click through to get to checkout, where other offers are left UNCHECKED but can be selected to add to their original purchase. Make it easy for them to move on and don't confuse them or you'll lose the sale.

Another effective way to implement this technique is called a "one- time-offer" or "OTO". This requires special software that presents the additional product(s) after the first one is purchased but not yet delivered. In this scenario, instead of a download or thank you page, you are delivered to a page which says, "Thank you for your order. Now, because you've just purchased product xyz, we have a special offer for you and don't close this page because you will lose that offer once you do. In other words you will never have another chance to take advantage of this offer."

Then you make an offer for another, usually complementary product at a discount price. This add-on sale always increases your overall sales and many people report that up to 50% or more take the OTO. So, imagine you sell the main product for $27 and then offer the resale rights to the product as an OTO for an additional $27, normally $47. So, instead of a $27 sale, you've now made a $54 sale.

Why not offer the resale rights for $54 upfront instead? Because testing has shown that you'll get a lot more sales with the OTO than asking for the $54 at the start. You see, they've already bought the $27 product. Now, it's just a small extra amount and that is more likely to get accepted.

So, let's say you make 100 sales at $27, that's $2700. With the OTO, you make an additional $1350 for a total sales of $4050, assuming a 50% OTO rate.

You can also do the same by offering a complementary product instead of resale rights. You can offer the OTO at a higher price, called an up- sell, or at a lower price, called a down-sell.

To get your OTO offer to truly appear once and only once, you'll need special software. There are a couple ways to do this.

You could hire a programmer at one of the outsource sites like Elance.com or RentACoder.com or you can purchase an already programmed and much more elegant solution like Rapid Action Profits.

If you go with RapidActionProfits, you'll be able to do a lot more as well since they have an add-on system where you can add features as they are developed.

Timing this strategy

There are several different times when this strategy is effective. You can set it up immediately so that a very simple offer is made available on the home page. Make sure to change this offer for repeat visitors. The idea is to start to form a habit by having someone be tempted to buy a small item immediately. So, that's the first time you want to try to slip your visitors into a buying groove.

The second time to use it is after they've already committed to buying a small item and they are checking out. This can be done automatically using software that adds a footer with additional items that might interest your buyer, or an additional page to move through to get to the final checkout.

Mesmerize with something new

In a consumer culture saturated with products for sale everywhere, you have to distinguish what makes your offering better than everyone else's offering. This can be difficult to do if you are selling brooms or something so ordinary that the market has been completely saturated with ads talking about the benefit of brooms or some other item. People become jaded or bored with these ads and can't really justify to themselves why one broom is better than another. After all, they all sweep floors.

That's when you want to try and see your product's unique personality and bring it out into the open where it can be appreciated. Now, that's slick marketing to take something old and make it new again. Not only that, but maybe your product has some benefits that the other products truly don't have. You can polish those up and mention them in your copy too, to differentiate yourself on the market.

The strategic plan

Okay, let's pretend you have a bunch of office supplies you are trying to sell online. You want to get into the mindset of your customers as much as you can. Why would they come online to buy office products? Why are they choosing to buy some products and not others? What is unique about a particular product that can give it a competitive edge? You can even gear your product's unique qualities to the audience you've targeted.

For instance, say you are using Social Ads on Facebook to target a particular demographic of people for your office supplies. Well, Facebook and other social networking sites attract people who want to communicate their identities. So, you may decide to sell office products that can be personalized to suit a person's personality. Whatever the market is, that's the one you are looking to sell to. Keep that in mind.

Try to use strategies that are different from your competitors and that play up your offerings. For instance, if you are selling martial arts courses, you don't want to only list those benefits that everyone else has on their website, you want to make sure you include extra benefits.

While other people may throw out statistics on how many women are assaulted by someone they know, you might opt to go less of the scare tactic route. Instead, you may want to differentiate your courses by stating how easy they are to learn online and how they can help you develop fitness while keeping you safe. So, that way even though there is a whole market of people who may be looking to do martial arts for safety, that's not the only reason. It may be people who are interested in Asian martial arts forms or fitness who you are engaging online.

That's the beauty of online marketing, the audience is very wide open. You are going to have people world-wide who show up to visit your site and you can't assume you know that the sole reason they are looking at your martial arts courses online is because you are afraid for your safety, even if that is the case. You can always add these benefits, but don't forget to add the other benefits too!

The psychological triggers

The key here is that most people need a reason to say yes. That's why salespeople sell benefits and not products. Ask any good salesperson and they will tell you that the benefits and unique characteristics of the product is what eventually sells it, even if the marketer is the one highlighting these qualities. People generally don't buy things they don't need, but they will need a reason to say yes, even if they do need the product.

The reason for this is that people are constantly pressured in this consumerist society to buy, buy, and buy. At some point, they either become jaded or tune out. When they tune out, it's the marketer's responsibility to help them tune back in. The customer may even be in desperate need of your product, but they may not be aware of it – they are so tuned out. It is your job to slowly bring them back in and educate them about why they need your product.

How to implement effectively

Because your customer may not be aware of their need for your product, you will have to give them time to realize it. This is not a fast way to make a sale, but it is a way to convert visitors into customers, eventually. Once they are your customer, they will be so convinced of your product's unique qualities and benefits, they will be hard-pressed to go elsewhere for their needs. So, you are not just converting a visitor, but you are also promoting your brand and establishing familiarity and authority with your products.

So, don't be upset if you don't make a sale right away. This strategy takes patience. You can hit on a few customers who have an eureka moment when you first start listing your benefits, but mostly people need to hear or read things multiple times for it to have an impact.

Then, something can happen in their lives that suddenly shifts their attention back to all those benefits you've been listing on your website or products for years. Maybe they didn't think they needed to supplement their diet, but now they are turning older and people around them are getting forgetful. Maybe they are noticing they are more forgetful too. Suddenly, they remember that one of the benefits of Gingko Biloba, a supplement you are selling, listed the benefits of memory enhancement. All of a sudden, the product is more appealing. And, the thing is you never know when that eureka moment will happen with the visitors to your website, so you have to keep copy up listing each product's unique qualities to help educate them for when the need actually arises.

So, remember to remind your customers often on the benefits of a particular product, even if they've seen the benefit on other pages. Repetition is important with this strategy. You want to be able to slowly, but surely gain the attention of someone who is hearing the same message from various sources until it finally sinks in. That's why when you develop a new product, you don't just want to put one sales page up, but you want to write articles, introduce it to various people at the same time through groups, discussion forums, or even paid reviews. They need to hear about this product over and over again until they finally see a need for it in their lives. When that happens, it's totally up to the consumer.

A great way to implement this strategy and make instant sales is with items that can bring out the inner child in people, like electronics. People love computers, cell phones, flat-screen TVs, and other types of electronic wizardry because it mesmerizes them with technology and also brings out the impulse to play around with their new purchase. Anytime you have a product like that, you can make instant sales and they can be very high priced, in comparison to older products in your inventory. So, even though this strategy can work for any product, in order to get it to work instantly, you want to use it most with products that have an instant mesmerizing effect on people. Things that are tactile and produce an experience of child- like wonder or playfulness are excellent products to use with this strategy.

Software is also something that can be sold quite well with this strategy and allow a person to get a small experience of the larger product either with a free trial or a limited demo-like experience. If your software is for games or like a game, this too can bring out the impulse to play and produce the desired effect to influence your potential buyer to want to possess this new toy.

Timing this strategy

This timing to sell the benefit or the product's unique personality is when they land on your sales page. You should have a sales page that funnels people from a blog, your signature, or other places to where they actually see all the benefits that make your product truly unique. You should set the title of your sales page to include the BIGGEST, and MOST IMPORTANT benefit that you want to highlight about your product or service. Many people don't get past that first title before moving away from the page, so make it count. It should highlight your product's unique nature while being something that is attractive to the majority of people who might land on your sales page.

The second instance of using this strategy is directly underneath the title. Just list every last benefit you can possibly think of for your product or service. Many online marketers think that the longer your sales page is and the more benefits you list, the more likely you will hit one that eventually produces that eureka moment in the customer. Just be sure to ask for the sale several times on the same page too, so that if they do happen to find that reason to buy that overcomes all their objections, they don't have to scroll too far to see the link to buy too.

Lastly, you can also start to keep a file of one-line benefits for each product you are selling. Add that to your signature and rotate them so that your signature changes constantly and people reading your emails see a new benefit every time they read one of your emails. Don't forget to include links to the sales page too here.

Another time to implement it is when you have multiple items in your inventory. You can highlight newer products over the others by showing how this new product has definite benefits over the other ones. The nice thing about new products is that they often can be higher priced and still sell. Think of when a new style of cell phone comes out. These types of electronic products fascinate people with the way they can push buttons, take pictures, send text mails, and endless other features. And, the price is usually quite high for a new cell phone on the market because demand is expected to be high too. So, when you highlight a new product in your inventory, you also have the potential to make higher priced sales too.

The overall timing on this strategy is sometimes up to the customer, not the marketer. You can constantly remind people why your products are unique, but it's up to them to finally connect their need to your product. However, this dynamic shifts when the market environment makes your products far more attractive, like when there is a drought and you happen to have rain barrels.

You may have spent years telling everyone that rain barrels save you money by helping them to store water and use it for their landscaping needs. However, if there is no drought, the fact that people have to buy them and install them without a perceived need, can make them difficult to sell. With the drought, you will see your demand skyrocket, because now you can also add: "Don't let the drought kill all your valuable landscaping, buy a rain barrel." See? Your product didn't change, even your benefit did not change, but the environment for the sales changed dramatically, making the timing perfect for selling rain barrels.

Mine your sales prospect's unconscious desires

In this strategy to turn your Internet traffic into paying customers, you want to concentrate on the person buying, the sales prospect, rather than the product. Your sales prospects can determine what lures will work best for you in converting visitors to customers, but for that you really have to understand your demographics.

If you haven't done some sort of market research in your demographics, you will want to do that. In face-to-face interactions, the demographics are the people you visit to market with your products, but online it is not as obvious who is visiting your site and why. So, you will want to gather some information through surveys, hiring market research for demographics, checking out the statistics of your website logs, and also using social networking to get a better feel for who might be interested in your products.

The strategic plan

To understand the unconscious desires that may be lurking in a sales prospect's mind, you need to interact with them and start to get to know them. Some people do this with surveys, by offering a freebie in exchange for visitors filling out a survey. However, that's not going to give you a full view as many people refuse to fill out surveys. So, the next option is to get the people who visit to interact in a forum or group where you can ask questions, see what people are talking about, and get a general feel for who is showing up to your website.

So, start out by gathering information on anything that might appeal to your customer. In social networking places like Facebook, this is a pretty simple thing to do. You just look through the profiles that people draw up in a network and that tells you a lot about what motivate people who join certain groups on Facebook. But, you also have to direct your market research to your product interest too.

So, say you are trying to find out the subconscious motivations of people who are visiting your pet site. There are the obvious reasons that they are interested in pets and pet products. But, that doesn't determine the subconscious motivation that may get them to buy your pet products. For that, you might want to know more about your visitors. Do they have hobbies? Are they having safety issues? What about where they live, is there something there that might make it more appealing to have pets or more important to have pet products?

At the end of your research into this issue, you may come up with a couple of different ways to implement the strategy, once you have a good idea of some underlying motivations that might be driving traffic to your website.

Then, you simply provide the solution to this unconscious desire by providing services that match your target market's needs. You will want to do that by writing online copy that expresses how it solves their needs, by selling the benefits first. But, if you have done your homework well, you will be pushing a trigger button that gets immediate attention and can result in an instant sale purely from understanding the psychology of why your customers buy.

The psychological triggers

Let's face it, when it comes to subconscious triggers most people are on automatic pilot. Our entire society is set up to keep people in this hypnotic state, so people generally don't question why they do a certain thing or make a particular purchase, they just may have the vague sense they need it. However, there are some subconscious triggers that appeal to almost everyone's egos: sex, money, and power. These are not so hidden, except that when people make a purchase, they may not even be aware that it is exactly one of these triggers that finally sealed the deal.

That's why advertisers showcase pretty girls with their products for men. They may be selling electric shavers, but the woman is the one touching his face on television and going: "Aaah!" Right? Isn't that so? So, was it the features of that particular razor that sold it or the subconscious trigger that insinuated that the person's sex appeal would shoot up dramatically if they used it? Probably the latter. However, if you ask a person why they bought that razor, they will most likely start to tell about the features because the trigger was so subconscious they don't even realize they were influenced by it.

Then, there are subconscious triggers that aren't so universal but are specific to your demographic and your product. For instance, do you remember the commercials about the elderly person who falls and can't get up? Then, they have the instant communication system around their neck that notifies someone they need help. Okay, so what is the subconscious trigger here? It's the fear of living alone and having no one around to help. That might be specific to the demographic of the elderly people they were trying to sell. But, no matter how memorable the commercial is, most people buying it would probably not want to admit that fear of being frail or even being elderly, for that matter. They might convince themselves that the reason they bought it was because it was convenient or not that expensive.

So, be aware that the unconscious desires can be universal or specific to your demographic. The key is to provide the solution or associate your product with that unconscious desire so that people will feel more compelled to close the deal.

In a way, you will have to be smarter than the people who are buying your products. You may have a product that doesn't appear to have universal appeal, but you want to use this strategy. It's your job to figure out a way to associate that product with either sex, money, or power or some other unconscious desire that may land you a sale.

How to implement effectively

To implement this strategy online, you will not only be targeting sales, but any call to action that can increase the value of your website or blog. In these terms, a call to action may be to buy something, but it can also be to add a comment to your blog, to discuss something in a public forum, to join your email list, or any other action that makes the buyer interact with the site. If you have a lot of activity on your site, this can help you define what is motivating the visits to your site and how to manifest your visitors' unconscious desires, as we talked about earlier.

You will want to use the gathering phase to cull information on your visitor's subconscious desires. Maybe you experience more sales from people who are visiting your site from the Southern United States in the summer than you do from other regions of the country. That tells you that there is something specific to that region that is motivating sales. The fact is that Southern states have a harder time controlling fleas in the summer months and even though you may not live there, your website is worldwide and people have found it and are buying. Well, one of the ways you can influence a subconscious trigger is just to advertise how many Southerners actually buy from your site, but that's not very subtle. It may trigger feelings of belonging and also status too, but it can also make them wonder why they're being targeted.

The key to using a subconscious trigger is to keep it somewhat subconscious. You may get it, but it shouldn't be too obvious to the people who are buying your products or they will resist it.

So, maybe you find out people in the South who have lots of dogs or cats living in the country and like country music or NASCAR.

Voila! You set up your pet site with a referral from a country music star or a NASCAR driver. You don't mention the word "south" at all, even though that's your demographic. You don't say that Southerners have too many fleas in the summer, you just have your celebrity showing how effective it is to treat their pets with your product and what they like about it (the benefits).

The subconscious trigger of identity is very powerful. They will identify your product with where they live, in the South, and probably think of you more in association with the celebrity. Every time they hear a song or watch NASCAR, subconsciously they will remember that ad and if they happen to be doing it in the summer, you've probably already made a sale.

So, the thing is to be subtle but focused on your product and target audience when you are going to close the deal. That doesn't mean that you can't use this strategy for other things to get your visitors involved in your site and help you determine their needs. As mentioned earlier, a valid action on your site might be someone putting a comment on your blog or adding a post to a discussion group on your site. If your site is a group site with membership levels and more, you can easily use the subconscious desire to belong to stimulate growth in your website and more activity. You can even sell memberships on your site if you target the subconscious desire to belong to a status group very carefully.

The way to do this is to build a core group first, of people who are already online. This gives your site authority. Then, use strategies like Facebook where people join who have similar networks, interests, or because they are friends already. So, you sign up people, and invite them to have their friends join. You can even give them something for their effort, by either using a point system or some free gift. This will help you build a network of people with similar interests who want to buy your products.

Another way to use the subconscious desire to belong is to add different membership levels to your site. This works particularly well for sites that have a great deal of prestige. EBay uses this strategy by offering sellers a Powerseller status on their membership if they happen to have a high number of sales and a 98% feedback rating by the end of several months. If they do, they are automatically promoted to Powerseller status.

Meanwhile, this motivates people to sell a lot and keep up good customer service on eBay. Similarly, if you own a respected research or non-profit site, you can have people who want memberships to get different perks per membership level and different types of recognition for being a part of your organization. This helps you sell memberships and increases your pool of people.

Timing this strategy

The timing for this is actually very flexible. You can influence people through their subconscious programming at any stage of the sales cycle. It is particularly effective at the beginning when people might be attracted to your website, but not quite identifying it with their needs yet. By carefully triggering those subconscious desires they will associate your website, and products, with the solution to their needs. So, while you can do this anytime, at the beginning it can form a powerful first impression without being overbearing or insulting to the buyer's intelligence.

Another time that is perfect for this strategy is on your membership sales page, since you can trigger the particular subconscious reasons someone might join and help them to seal the deal. For instance, maybe you are a non-profit that deals with environmental cleanup, then you can have on your membership page the different levels and how each level helps you to do more good in the community. You can send them a bumper sticker or some other personally identifying perk to make them proud they belong to such a wonderful organization.

Also, when a deal has already been closed, you might still be able to use a subconscious trigger right before the checkout to get more sales. Like the Amazon list that shows "people who bought this item also bought these" which triggers a status subconscious desire. How can you pass up the other books when so many other people have them? Are they smarter than you? Richer than you? What do they know that you don't know? So, you might get triggered to buy more just to keep up with the Jones.

Spot the flaws first

If you ask a salesperson whether an objection to their sales presentation is bad, you'll get the answer: "No." A good sales person knows that with any presentation or marketing, objections will arise. That's a good thing because once an objection is raised by the sales prospect, most marketers can resolve it and dismiss it, leaving the way clear to buying their product. So, objections typically are raised by the customer in most sales transactions, but this strategy is done by the seller and not the potential buyer. That's right, you will be the one raising the objections so that you can just as swiftly dismiss them and get to the closing.

The reason this particular strategy is important in online marketing is because you are not interacting with the potential buyer face to face. They visit your site, find something they like, and like any reasonable customer they will start to think of reasons they shouldn't buy it. That's just what most people do; they resist being marketed. So, if your product has any obvious flaws that's exactly the first objection that will be raised in their mind. Maybe the product is ugly, or it costs too much, or it's gotten bad reviews. Don't wait for the customer to raise that objection in their own minds and click away, instead you raise it first! So, for instance, if you know your product costs more than all the competitors, raise that first by saying: "Our product costs more because it's better than the competition!" And, then go on to use that as a lead into the benefits.

The strategic plan

The strategy is to disarm your buyer by bringing up the objection first, before they even have time to think about it or utter it in their minds. This works whether the product has some faults or not, but it is especially effective with those that have obvious faults. Don't believe that a buyer will miss a flaw with the product or that if you concentrate on only highlighting the good qualities that the bad qualities won't be noticed. Consumers are very sophisticated these days.

Online retailing has made it incredibly easy for them to comparison shop without having to visit multiple stores. Some sites even have reviews of products online that tell them which kinds are the best. Of course, magazines like consumer reports will tell buyers what basic features they can expect from a product and what makes one a better deal than another. It's a bit naive to think that you will have a totally uninformed consumer drop by your website and not notice anything that is obviously flawed about your product. That doesn't mean you can't bring that up first and either make it a feature or find a way to resolve that objection that satisfies them as fair.

The psychological triggers

When you bring up an objection first it has a couple of effects. First, it makes you appear to be honest and forthright because you willingly brought up the subject first. It also decreases the resistance your buyer may have to the objection because you've reframed it in a way that acknowledges the flaw, but gives them a way to justify it. So, by simply being willing to be upfront, you can undercut the objection before it happens. This is a way of disarming the reaction of the buyer by simply acknowledging the concern upfront.

If, on the other hand, you took the tact of trying to avoid the flaw and hoping they didn't see it, you would appear to be deceitful and the person would lose confidence in the sale. If you brought up the flaw, but minimized it as a valid objection, your buyer will wonder what else is wrong with your product that you don't think is worth mentioning. But, if you bring up the flaw, acknowledge it, and then resolve it for them in a way that they can justify the purchase, you close the deal.

In a way, the buyer is more likely to trust the rest of the presentation because you didn't gloss over the bad features of your product. Since you were honest enough to be upfront, that lends you credibility and that credibility rubs off on the product, whether it deserves it or not. And, when you go on to actually talk about the positive features they are given more weight, because you were honest with the negative ones. While you might think people would be turned off by acknowledging a defect, hiding it under the rug is a worse offense in most people's minds.

How to implement effectively

This is something that you should consider when you have a product or service with an obvious flaw. So, let's say that you are trying to sell used tires. Okay, used tires are obviously not as good as new tires, are they? Well, you can't advertise the tire like new tires. So, you admit – hey, they're used tires.

Then, you can go on to say that despite the fact they are used tires and not brand new, they are checked to make sure they have sufficient tread on them, they pass some inspection for holes etc., you offer a guarantee should they not last a certain amount of miles, and you can still offer the same brands that other retail people sell brand new. Oh, and don't forget that if they're used, you save money too because the price is lower for the same name brands.

This works very well if you are selling items on eBay and they are not new or they have some obvious defect. You want to be completely upfront with that defect. It should be the very first thing you discuss, so that there is absolutely no misunderstanding that the product may be perceived to be flawed by other standards. The worse thing that can happen online is that your customer gets a product delivered to them that doesn't match the description on your website. You can expect them to not only never buy another thing from your site, but on eBay and places that allow your customer's to provide feedback, you will get negative feedback and scare other customers away. However, that doesn't mean that you can only sell new products that are in perfect mint condition online.

Far from it! It means that you need to be explicit about the condition of the items that you are selling and very upfront about them.

Another way to implement this is to offer a limited guarantee on the product. That way, if the person is completely unsatisfied, they can return it or get some form of compensation for their troubles. This is one way to dismiss many objections people might have about buying items that aren't new or in perfect condition.

Unfortunately, online, people don't always read every piece of copy you put up about your product. However, they do usually read the very first part of the copy before scrolling down. It seems strange, but that's where you will put the acknowledgement of the defect. If you bury it elsewhere in the copy and get an order and the customer becomes irritated, directing them to the online copy where your flaw is buried two-thirds of the way down the page is going to make them even madder.

On the other hand, if you say, "Yeah, this piece of art is BUTT- UGLY...", it's a great way to get attention and dismiss the worst defect you have on the product. Maybe the piece of art you are auctioning is butt-ugly, however, it's also one of a limited collection of prints made by a celebrated artists and worth hundreds of dollars! The customer scrolling through eBay or your site will initially be shocked to see that you actually admit that this product you are selling has an obvious flaw. They may even find it humorous. It will definitely get their attention, and that will lead them to read the rest of the copy which explains all the other benefits and how you can dismiss the defect as either part of the charm of the piece or as not consequential to its actual value.

Don't be afraid to get down the real nitty gritty details of why the product is flawed. Maybe it's ugly because it has too many loud colors. Maybe it's ugly because it has drab colors. Maybe it's ugly because it's abstract or too primitive. Whatever the problem is, be very clear that you understand that this is something that most people would consider an undesirable trait. Then, go on to dismiss it by building up the positive benefits of the product immediately afterwards. You are dismissing the flaw either by addressing the concern directly or you are going to show that despite this flaw the benefits of the product far outweigh the flaw mentioned.

This strategy is often used by real estate agents when they show houses with obvious flaws. They might point out the fact that the house is a little older than desired by their client, but the location is so good that the money they save in buying an older house can be used to update it and then they have both a good location and a newer home. They might show off the carpet with badly stained carpets and tell their buyers that since the carpets are so badly stained they can ask for a carpet allowance and put in whatever they want after they move it, making it their own.

The trick here is to do this as people are considering buying your product, not as an introduction, but as part of the description of the item. Obviously, this strategy is best left to the actual sales page than as a way to introduce a product to people on online forums or discussion groups. It's for people who already have a good idea that they want to buy in this category and that they may have some decisions to make on whether a flaw that is apparent is a deal- breaker or not.

Timing this strategy

The time to bring up a default is not after you've sold them on the benefits, but before. It should be brought up immediately before the person has time to discover it themselves, but not as an introduction to people who haven't had a chance to discover your site yet. It's like the difference between seeing a house on the market and wanting to visit it and being at the door of a house and opening the door to actually experience it.

If you are imagining the house from afar, if you start to talk about the flaws even before you've visited it, the value of the house plummets and you're less likely to visit the house. You haven't had a chance to experience it so that the better characteristics of the house can outweigh the flaw. So, don't mention these items unless they are already in an area where they have an option to buy and can have a full experience of the product you are offering it.

Then, it's more like you are there with the potential buyer and they are walking through the door as a real estate agent to show them your property that is for sale. If you are walking into a house as a real estate agent, you can say, "the appliances are old, but you can always ask for an appliance upgrade if you like the house."

You don't wait until the person walks into the kitchen, stares at the appliances and then says: "The appliances are outdated!" If you've been in this house before, you should know the negatives, and it should be said as you're opening the door to let them in, preferably before they've even had a chance to see the kitchen. If you bring it up early in the experience (but not before they're actually there with you visiting the products), and in all its gory detail, they imagine something far worse and when they get to the kitchen they might even mutter, "It's not that bad!" That's because you are so upfront with them, that they realize it's not a big deal.

Online, you don't want to put all kinds of objections on your home page, but you do want the sales page to have them if you know there is a problem with the product. If you are doing eBay to make sales and using them as a sales partner, you will want to make sure it is in bold and a title heading at the top of the page. You don't want people to miss it and then end up with something they object to AFTER they've already paid for the item. That will only get you irate customers and negative feedback. So, the best timing is always right up front.

Convert problems into opportunities

If you do spot a problem with your product, you can dismiss it (as in the earlier example), or you can convert it into an opportunity. This strategy is a little more creative than the last one, where you are just being blunt about your dirty laundry. In this one, you are being truthful about the problem, but you are reframing it from a negative to a positive. Once people start to see that you may have a point, that negative really is a positive, then you don't even have to dismiss the objection, it becomes another selling feature.

So, you do have to raise the objection first, and use the strategy's we have already discussed, but you want to resolve the objection on a positive note. If you can be really creative and sell that problem as a feature, it can be a way to disarm and even charm people reading the copy on your website.

The strategic plan

The strategy involves learning how your potential buyers perceive your product and any objections they might raise in their own minds. You don't have to be a mind reader to figure that out. You can simply ask them. You can set up surveys that offer a discount coupon on your products or offers a freebie to get a little market research on particular products. You have to know which objections might be converted into opportunities, and often they may not even be objections that you would think about first.

You can even add a few posts about a product on some group site or your own forums and see what people don't like about the product as well as what they do like. Some of these objections may be specific to your particular product, but others might be pretty generic. For instance, say you are selling tattoo art online. Well, you obviously aren't the only one selling tattoo art designs and you can visit specialty groups and forums and find out what people are talking about. Maybe they think unicorn tattoos are lame, or there is a particular discussion on whether it's such a good idea to have a permanent design on your body or not. Maybe you hear about the bad reactions people got years later from some tattoo they got when they were younger. So, now the objection is that a tattoo is permanent.

However, it also happens to be the opportunity because tattoos are permanent. They don't rub off, they are unique and can highlight your personality or mark a particular moment or event in your life, and you will always have that remembrance. So, even though some people might perceive the fact that a tattoo as permanent as a problem later in life, it's what also makes it so attractive too. All you need to do is educate the person visiting your site on why it is more of an opportunity than a potential problem. For this, you can even suggest that some tattoos now come with ink that can be removed with a laser later.

In the case of tattoos, we have a generic problem that crops up that makes an excellent opportunity. However, there may actually be problems that are specific to your product. In the case of the earlier example of a piece of art that is terribly ugly, would you be able to make it an opportunity? It is possible with a little creativity. Aren't ugly works of art controversial and conversation starters? Maybe it represents a particular time period of style of art that is only recognized by discriminating art buyers. In that case, the fact that it's ugly is the opportunity to express exactly why you were savvy enough to buy the piece anyway. It shows you are a person who understands art and the value of a piece of work.

The psychological triggers

Even though the major part of this strategy is to reframe a negative into a positive, you don't want to try to force something that will never be. You don't want to try to convince the potential buyer of something that is ludicrous or a stretch to believe because people are pretty smart about that sort of thing. So, you are reframing the objection into a positive, but in a way that is believable.

In another way, if you happen to reframe something that would normally appear negative into a positive in a bright and refreshing way, people will be surprised at first. That surprise lowers their resistance to believing the new way the problem has turned into an opportunity. Again, by raising the objection first, you have gotten the upper hand. You have set the stage to be the authority on this particular problem and you have guided the potential buyer to a solution that not only resolves the problem, but presents them with a great opportunity too.

At first, it will stir up feelings of shock that you dared to bring up the problem first, then it will lend you credibility and provide your voice with more authority on the subject. Finally, it will reduce their defenses and make it easy for them to go along with your final assessment of the problem as an opportunity. They will be grateful you actually pointed out something to them they just might have missed.

How to implement effectively

Okay, so you've done some market research and gotten a list of possible objections for your particular product or market. For each product, take out a sheet of paper and create two columns by running a line down the middle of an 8 1/2 X 11 sheet of paper. On the first side list all of the objections that you discovered or thought up, and then start to go through them one by one. You don't want to pick every objection and try to make it an opportunity. What that will do is make people think that there are far too many problems with the product and you're just messing with their minds. If you pick an objection that is not very serious to highlight, because it's easily converted into a positive, it will make you appear condescending instead of helpful.

If you pick something that isn't really an objection, you just think it might be able to be perceived as one, you are going to be raising an objection in your potential customer's mind that might never have surfaced. This will make them stop and think about what other red flags they've missed. So, you don't want to pick a weak objection or one that is non-existent. What you want to do is locate serious objections that people might have to your product and then creatively turn them into a positive. So, be careful which objections you consider to highlight as it can make or break this strategy.

Once you know which objections might qualify for this strategy, the fun starts. You have to be very creative and think up a resolution for each strategy that makes that problem an opportunity. There are some objections that are universal, not specific to your market or to your product. These are things like the price is too high, it takes too long to get it, it's not convenient, or the competition has better or different features.

Don't forget that you can target these objections as well and maybe you want to start with them for every product, just to get the hang of this. Then, you think up a reason for why that objection is really an opportunity. A classic example of this is when you have a product that is really expensive when compared to the competition. You can say it is a good value for the money because it offers more features than the competition too. So, while you pay more than the others, you get more and in the end it is worth more too.

This may be a little more "canned" in online presentation than in a regular face-to-face presentation. If you are meeting a sales prospect in person, you can often hear the objections live and/or anticipate them better from the comments they make. Online, you can't really interact that much with your visitor, so you have to take the strategy of doing your research and then picking just one of the biggest flaws and using that as a lead in for your sales page.

If you have multiple objections you want to resolve, then you can use a table that compares features between your product and other leading brands. Tables are very easy on the eyes of people reading online materials. So, they can see, that price-wise you are more expensive, but then the rest of the features are checked for you and your competitors columns are empty. This gives a very big visual impact and is a way of raising objections and resolving them without having to explain it out in a paragraph. The table is a visual tool that does it for you.

Always, always, always be upfront about any flaw or objection that is going to be a major concern for your customer. If you fail to address it, the potential buyers might bring it up or they might not, but they will surely be thinking about it. If you don't bring it up, it will never be resolved in their minds. An unresolved objection is going to dampen your sales. So, despite the fact that it may seem strange to be bringing up your product's bad points, it's far worse to not acknowledge them at all.

So, what happens if you are in the middle of a sales presentation and the product breaks or it doesn't perform the way you would expect it to? Acknowledge it right away and let people know the reason for that particular problem. Maybe you can bring up the fact that even if the product does not perform the way advertised, there is a guarantee they can use to get a replacement or something similar.

Sometimes people don't want to buy things online because they don't know what they're going to get when it arrives. This is particularly true of diamonds. The biggest objection a person buying a diamond online is how could they be sure the diamond they received was worth the thousands of dollars spent on it? So, many online diamond retailers raise that objection as a valid objection and showcase the fact that their diamonds are appraised by a particular agency. Or, they might discuss how the value is established and how safe the delivery is and any money back guarantees too. Now, the fact that you're buying a diamond online and may not be able to visually see it before it arrives and don't know how to determine worth is an opportunity to have a valid certification of your diamond for free through the website's policies.

Timing this strategy

The timing of this strategy is similar to the last strategy. Always bring up the objection first, before your customer has a chance to do it for you. You can shock them with the declaration of a particular problem. You can even not make it a statement, but a question. Like, "Are you afraid that you don't know if the diamond you buy online is worth what you paid for it?" That lead in will automatically bring people in because it acknowledges a fear that may lurk in the mind of the prospect but that has not be verbalized. Once you verbalize it, many people can relate to that fear and it draws their attention as being relevant to their personal experience. You come off looking as someone who is sympathetic and understanding for even bringing it up.

Then, when you provide the resolution, "Our diamonds are certified by third-party appraisals that are board-certified to be..." you not only have given them the prospective buyer the solution right away, but also relieved the fear and anxiety experienced with that particular problem. That sense of immediate anxiety and relief can end up leading to an instant sale.

You can do this very well in a targeted email campaign for those people who have subscribed to your email list. Don't spam people with advertisements, but if you are trying out a new product that most people have a problem buying online for some reason, you can use that niche to help you use this strategy by turning that objection into an opportunity. When presented correctly, it can be a way to engage the reader and draw them into your copy far enough for them to find the solution to their problem and associate your product with a new opportunity for themselves.

Engage participation and pride of ownership

People who get involved tend to be more committed to a particular path than those who are just visiting. This is true whether you are doing retail sales or online sales. However, in a face-to-face presentation people are naturally involved because a social interaction is taking place and they usually give you their full attention. Online, people may be surfing the web and be multitasking on their PCs. You don't know if you have their attention or not since you're not directly there to give them eye contact. So, how do you get them involved in your site if you can't reach out through their terminal and put the product in their hands?

Well, the solution is a lot easier than you think since social networking sites are now more predominant. Blogs, discussion groups, forums, and even surveys and games can be a way to engage the person to stop a moment and interact with your site. Once you've engaged their participation, they will start to identify with your site more. Now, if you get them to become a regular visitor who comments on your blog or has tried out some of your products, they start to feel like this is their home. They start to take pride in being part of your site and it can give them feelings like pride of ownership.

The strategic plan

Direct sales like mail marketing use something called an "involvement device" to get people involved over a long distance. That is something that they can touch and feel and that asks for some participation on their part. The one involvement device that comes to mind is some of the advertisements that ask you to peel a sticker from a particular part of the advertisement and place it somewhere else to signal your acceptance of the offer.

It seems very simplistic that having someone place a sticker or add a business card or drop something into a slot could ever increase sales, but it does. Once a person becomes involved in the sales process, they are more apt to pay attention and buy. Any device that engages the reader brings them into the buying process and reduces their resistance to the offer.

You don't just want to use any involvement device, you typically want to use something that ties into what you are selling. That's why Facebook applications are so popular because they are a great involvement devise that typically tie into the product or company and provide a way for people to associate their participation with some company or product. Then, if there is a link available back to the website, you are already primed to consider this a part of your virtual heritage.

Another type of involvement device is like the advertisements that ask you to draw a picture to see if you qualify for drawing lessons. You find that you get so involved in getting the picture done right, that you can hardly wait to mail it off and receive an offer for classes in the mail. Not only did those advertisers correctly identify people who might have an interest in buying art classes, but they also got them so involved they probably waited by the mailbox to see if they were accepted for this offer. That's very clever marketing!

The key there is that involvement device used was directly related to the product or services being sold. You can still use an involvement device that merely gets a person to participate, and online that would be like getting a comment on a blog. A person has taken some action that has gotten them involved in your community. But, did it make a sale? Not really, it might later, but not right away. So, the best involvement devices are those that are tied directly to the product or service you are trying to market.

The psychological triggers

Have you ever seen a baby find a new toy and become completely fascinated by it? It captures their attention and all their old toys get ignored while they explore this new object. They may put it in their mouths, stare at it intently, shake it, or even smash it on the floor. They get highly involved in just touching it and trying to get as much experience as they can out of it. Well, adults still have that fascination with new toys. And, that's part of the psychology of offering them something new that brings up that childish wonder of exploration.

The other thing is that people love to be challenged and to beat something and identify themselves as a winner. Some of the puzzles, games, and involvement devices can include different levels that differentiate your ability from other people and give you a sense of pride that you made it to a certain level.

Another way to involve people is to make it fun. Who doesn't want to include a little entertainment in their day? In fact, entertainment is one of the most sought-after things in our Western culture. If you happen to provide a fun involvement device that also happens to lead them to your product, all the better right? They get to have some fun and you end up with a sale, so in a sense, it's a win-win.

Also, people tend to distrust a product that they can't see, touch, or feel. So in direct retail sales, the involvement device is typically the ability to try on a dress before buying, kick the tires of a new car or test drive it, or even get a free make-over at a make-up department store booth. They want the experience of possessing the item before they actually purchase it.

These types of retail actions are simple ways to involve a person by just allowing them to touch and experience the product first-hand. This becomes a little harder in the virtual world of online sales because your product is not there to have and hold, but you can still produce some very good involvement devices and even virtual "visualize and experience" ads that can lead to bigger sales.

How to implement effectively

Since we are basically concerned with turning traffic from your website into customers, we want to really understand how to create an involvement device online. It's really not that hard, once you understand the concept. What you want to do is put yourself in the customer's shoes and see how you can get them engaged in at least visualizing themselves using your product or service.

In the first strategy, you can simply provide a novel and fun gimmick to your site to get them involved. If you are a dating site, for instance, you might want to add a compatibility test or personality test to your website. Once they complete that, you can sell the service by saying, "Find compatible people who match your personality on our site!" It not only gets them involved right away, but it appeals to ego identity, a large reason people join community sites.

Social networking is great for forming groups of people who can interact with each other. In a sense, the people on your site become the involvement device that attracts more people. If you are trying to sell memberships, you want to highlight who is already on your site and why it is worth it for you to join so you can network with them too.

If you really think about it, your entire website can be an involvement device. It has buttons people can push, drop-down menus they can fiddle with, and maybe videos they can watch. So, you can do the same thing when you are selling a particular product. Just be careful that you don't get too fancy. Some people try to involve their visitors by adding incredible technologies that look great on newer PCs, but can't be opened on older models! You don't want to lose a customer because the involvement device is too complicated or it crashes their system! You want something simple and you want it to appeal to the psychology more than the technology.

When you are marketing people offline, you can also provide involvement devices that lead back to your products online. There are now business cards that are mini CD-ROMs that can be loaded into a computer and lead people straight to your website. Just the fascination of seeing something so small, so cute, and so novel, will get people to put it in their machine to see what it does. Once they are on your site, you can involve them further with other involvement devices.

But, what if you're selling engagement rings online? How could you possibly create an involvement device for that? Won't someone want to try the ring on first before buying? Here is where you see the magic of the Internet really shine. You can hire a programmer to build a database of your inventory and an applet that allows them to build a ring online in the virtual world. Thus, they not only get the fun of creating something online, but they get to try out the ring too, in their imagination. It's the closest thing to actually being in a retail store where they can hold the ring in their hands. It may take a bit more programming and sophistication, but if your market demands a virtual try-out there are ways to do this, as many online diamond marketers have proven.

Your call to action can also include an involvement device or a fun game by allowing them some discount for performing a specific function on your site and thus getting access to a coupon code. Once they have that coupon code, wouldn't they want to use it to get the discount? So, you lead the potential buyer from their fun game straight back to your product or service.

Finally, even emails or sales copy can get the reader involved, if you happen to use the person's name in them and help them to imagine what it's like to experience your product. If you have a product that you can personalize, that also will give a person a feeling of pride of ownership before they've gotten the product in their hands. As can be seen, there are a great many ways to use this strategy online to help promote participation and involvement with your website and products.

Timing this strategy

This strategy works best at the very beginning of your sales funnel, or even before. You should have at least a few involvement devices on your website to help you create membership, if you are a social networking site. Otherwise, people lose interest in just writing posts and move on. If you have a fun game, or add a video from YouTube, when they first land on your page your website appears more interactive and alive.

Have you ever seen the sign on the side of the road as your waiting in a traffic jam that says: "You could live here."? That is a simple device that helps you imagine how much time you could save living there, how much nicer your life would be, and how you could own a condo there if you just took the initiative to walk in the door. That's a very powerful involvement device and it wasn't even in a sales brochure. You might not have even been thinking of buying a condo up until then. So, that explains that the timing on this strategy is sometimes even before the person has realized that your company even exists or what your products are.

You can wait for them to somehow stumble upon your site, but why not go out to places where people in your target demographic are and just put a link to your fun, experiential, involvement device there. You don't have to sell the product, you don't have to tell them at the end, they'll be solicited to buy a product. Once they choose to try this out, they will be hooked and you will have created a sales opportunity where none existed.

Once you have the person involved in the product, you can continue to keep them involved by upgrading the experience. This will create a habit, reducing their resistance to future purchases too. So, if you are using a game, make sure you have various levels. Keep the strategy going continuously and vary it every now and then to keep people involved and buying.

Be authentic to engender trust

In the past, marketers tried to glamorize their products or services in a way that was clearly inauthentic. The type of hype seems to have really jaded a lot of consumers who are pretty savvy these days. They are more likely to turn a deaf ear to outrageous claims or over-the- top commercial images than to pay attention. They do not engender trust. The newer way to generate trust is not to try and pull the wool over anyone's eyes, but rather to be authentic with our product and who you are.

In the age of social networking, more and more people are beginning to learn the value to their social reputation. A reputation that is misrepresented is one that is not trustworthy. If a person is not trustworthy, they do not have enough credibility to sell anyone in such a transparent environment. What will happen is that others in the social network will appear to warn people about the lack of authenticity and their social reputation will plummet along with their sales.

Now, you can be authentic without necessarily being a squeaky, clean, moralist. Authenticity basically means that you have enough integrity to express things exactly as they are. If you are a person who sells diet advice but can't be bothered to control your own diet, that lack of integrity is going to come back to bite you in a social networking situation. However, if you are authentic and say that you could never stay on any diet and didn't see the reason for them, and then you found this diet and it helped you lose 50 pounds, then you are being authentic. Thus, it becomes more and more important to believe in the products and services you are selling, to be able to report on them authentically and engender trust.

The strategic plan

Consistency is the buy word here. If you are consistent in your words and actions, then you become more authentic and can be trusted more. We've all had the experience of seeing someone say one thing and do another. What impression does that leave? You immediately realize that the person is a hypocrite or a con, at worst, or doesn't know what they're talking about, at best. So, to avoid giving off that impression, always make sure that your actions match your words. This goes for the way you describe you, your product, and to how well you keep your promises to the people buying from your site.

One way to establish authenticity is to either bank on your own reputation or someone else's well-known reputation.

You build a reputation through social networking that carefully represents the image you want for your company or product. Or, if you don't want to go through all that trouble, you find ways to associate with people who have already done that, have a high degree of credibility, and then get them to endorse your product or services.

Be clear about whether all your copy, all your products, and your public image are in line with the way you want people to perceive you. If you genuinely believe in what you are selling, that will come through and people will catch your enthusiasm simply from the power of your own self-trust. However, the same is true if you are careful with the copy or the image you are portraying. If you sell diet products and you are 50 pounds overweight, people will notice it, even if not consciously. You don't want to put your image on that website if you are seriously overweight because it shows you aren't being authentic about helping people lose weight.

So, much of this strategy is about being aware. Be aware what image you are projecting. Be aware what topics or writing is subconsciously influencing your potential buyer. Be sure that anything you associate with, whether it be a celebrity or an affiliate be in line with that image you want for you and your products. Secondly, always, deliver more than what you promise and your authenticity and integrity score will shoot through the roof.

The psychological triggers

If you are engaging in online marketing and you are trying to sell products or services without even knowing a potential prospect, the need for authenticity increases. It has taken quite a bit of time for people to begin to trust e-commerce, and many of the reasons for that is because of the potential for being conned online. Visitors will be trying to gage your authenticity from every piece of email, copy, blog, or image they view. They want to know that you are trustworthy enough to deliver what you say you deliver. After all, no one wants to send money and either get nothing, or a very bad product in return. Since, they can't even touch the product they are requesting, it becomes more important they trust the vendor enough to deliver what they promise.

When you go retail shopping, you can look into someone's eyes and get a good feel for whether someone is trying to con you or not. The cues for that behavior may be subtle, but people have a sixth sense about these things. They want that firm handshake, that eye-to-eye contact, that honesty, and that ability to resolve their issues for them. In addition, they like to be able to view a product before they actually buy it. They might want to touch it or try it out first too. Well, when all of that is denied, they have to rely on someone else's word for whether they are engaging in a good transaction or whether they are just throwing money away. In order to relieve that anxiety, you implement the strategy to increase your level of authenticity to promote a sense of mutual trust. But how are you going to do that online when they can't even see your face, much less touch the product?

How to implement effectively

The key is in the subtle cues that are given off by all your interactions with a potential buyer. Make sure that every one of your interactions reflects exactly the image you want for your company, your products, or your services. Things to look for in your copy or interactions that could set off doubts in your buyers mind are things like over- exaggerating your product's benefits or speaking out of context from the image you want to portray. The best way to avoid some of these subtle patterns of speech that can trigger doubts about your authenticity is to pay attention or to avoid marketing anything you don't believe in 100%.

Let's face it, if you are selling acne products and you've either never tried it (because you never experienced a bad outbreak) or you tried it and it failed to work for you, when you go to sell that product, the lack of enthusiasm and belief will shine through the choice of words, the images you use, and any other interaction. It's a part of you and despite the fact that you may try to convince yourself that this is really a product that is worth marketing, because acne products sell well on the Internet, you will find that if you don't believe in it, your words and interactions will take on a subtle tone of over- exaggeration or bland endorsements. Worse, when someone contacts you directly to ask you what your experience was with the product, you may even have to outright lie to save face.

This isn't to suggest that you shouldn't sell that particular acne product, the problem is the way you implement the strategy. If you are endorsing it personally, you are going to want to have some good experiences with the product to remain authentic while selling it. If you are simply choosing acne products as your main market, then you can include it with other acne products that you know do work and simply rate it lower than the others or leave it unrated. That way you maintain a degree of authenticity while being able to promote more products. And, you may find a way to engage your visitors by asking them to rate the products themselves for others. Then, you not only get authenticity from unpaid for reviews, but you didn't have to put up your own reputation in the process.

Forms of this strategy are the celebrity sponsor who tells everyone that they've used your products and like them. Just be sure it is a celebrity that reflects your values and the product's proper image. If your celebrity just got convicted of dog fighting racketeering charges, you would not want them endorsing your pet products.

Social networking also takes this strategy to new heights. If you have a discussion group or forum, and you have a new product, you can offer the product out to the first 10 people who ask for it, in exchange for a review of it on site. Since many discussion groups, social networking sites, and forums have a large audience, you end up picking up a great deal of authenticity by using random people who will give their honest opinion on your products. Just be sure they are good products and good reviews.

Timing this strategy

The timing for this is right in the middle of your sales presentation. Once your sales prospect is engaged and they are a loyal visitor to your site or a subscriber to your blog, endeavor to be consistent and trustworthy in all your interactions. This will help to keep people coming back again and again.

Another time to use this is when you are putting out brand new products. There, you have to attract new sales and banking on your reputation is one way to help spur the belief that this new product is just as good, if not better than your other products. Engage others to review your product too and this will help to spur sales. Capitalize on the authentic image you've already created with your past customers. That's the time to market people who already trust you by making sure they are updated on all the new products that you are selling. This can lead to many repeat sales.

Finally, the best way to establish authenticity is to deliver what you promise, when you promise it. Some people try to do this even better by always delivering more than they promise and earlier than expected. That gives them a little leeway should the post office screw up the timing or something else happens. So, if you want to be perceived as being truly authentic strive to take control of all aspects of your business from delivery to customer support. Failure in any of these areas will reduce your authenticity because it reflects badly on the consistency of the promises you make and what is finally delivered.

If you want to see if your authenticity is being questions, simply send out customer satisfaction surveys on a regular basis or after an online transaction. These are pretty easy to implement on your site and can help you find areas that are not meeting the high standards of consistency that you want to maintain.

You can have these collated monthly for review and/or endeavor to contact people who put in negative feedback immediately, without delay. This helps to reduce the impact of any failure in your consistency and can even increase your authenticity if you manage to resolve a problem that has plagued a customer who didn't know what to do or who to contact to resolve the issue. It also shows you care about your customers.

Enchant with stories

If you've ever heard the story of 1,001 Arabian Nights, you know the power of stories to enchant the listener. That's because people are hard-wired to myth for ancient times. They want to hear things spoken in story form and their subconscious has a way of remembering what they hear in story form better than visual cues. If you use stories in your marketing, you will not only capture people's attention, but you will also help them to remember you long after they've left your website.

The other aspect of stories that enchants people is the capacity to create empathy and communion with the story-teller. How many of us remember asking our parents to read a bedtime story? Wasn't it a special time of bonding for us? The same can be true of stories that you tell when you are trying to establish a rapport with people coming to your website.

The strategic plan

The strategy is to try to capture a person's attention by initiating a story that fascinates them into a longer relationship with you. Obviously, they will not leave until they've heard the punch line or found out how the story ended. The story should have some human elements in it, so that your reader can relate to it on a personal level. If it is just a story of a product, without some human element, it will sound like hype. So, be careful to include your product or service in the story, but don't make it a story solely about that product.

The story should try to stir the reader's curiosity from the get go. It is this sense of "what's going to happen" that will lead the reader, deeper and deeper into your story. It can be a story about some people's experience with your product. It can be a story about the development or discovery of your product. It can even be a humorous story about your product. It really doesn't matter, as long as you are engaging the reader in a deeper relationship and connection with your product or service.

The way you know if the strategy is working is if you can get the reader to read the entire story to the very end, where the sales pitch is. Once they have become so involved in the story line, they will empathize with the actors in the story, identify with the product and their own predicaments, and be very likely to consider buying the product right then and there. That's the power of a good story. It breaks down the resistance to buying, much like a set of benefits does too.

But, in this case, it works more subconsciously than consciously, which makes it a far more powerful strategy in the long run. They may leave your website and three hours later still remember that story and thus, they will also remember your product better. The deeper the impact of a story, the more likely the reader will remember your products when they have a need or are looking for a solution like your story relates.

The psychological triggers

Storytelling involves telling jokes as well as long, drawn-out stories with a beginning, middle, and end. They work to lessen the awkwardness of a social encounter, especially between people who have never met before. If you can get a person to laugh at your joke or identify with your story, you become more familiar to them and less of a stranger. The impact of a story is only as good as how well it causes the reader to bond with the storyteller and be drawn into the final conclusion of the story.

Jokes are very easy to reel off at the beginning of a sales encounter, but they are much more difficult to enact well. It takes a certain flare to be able to tell a joke well so that it comes out humorous and not lame. However, jokes are brilliant ways to tell a tiny story in a very small amount of time and have people bond with you through the mechanism of humor and laughter. It builds a warm camaraderie and can help you establish mutual trust from the onset.

However, if you're not good at telling jokes, telling a personal account or story can be another great way to bond with your website visitors. It brings the human element to the forefront of your website and humanizes the technological aspect of being online. It appeals to the subconscious triggers within a person and can be a subtle way to manipulate the unconscious desires or fears they may be experiencing to help them make the decision to buy.

How to implement effectively

Online stories can involve all sorts of media from written copy, to cartoons, or video blogs. If you have a good short story that can be made into a video, you can add that to YouTube to try to make it go viral. It can be a story that relates your product as the solution to an embarrassing event with the title, "Don't let this happen to you!" At the end, you put a link to your website to draw that traffic to your sales page. That's the way to use a video and the power of the Internet to create a sales page story line. It can be very powerful if plenty of people relate to it or find it humorous, as it can be spread across the Internet very quickly if it has mass appeal.

Another way to use a story is through written copy on your website. Maybe the story has a lesson to teach about why your product is the solution to a particular dilemma. Maybe you want to relate a humorous story about your product that is entertaining for the reader. Maybe you want to give the reader the opportunity to experience an "ah-ha" moment that some other customer had when they used your product or service. It really doesn't matter what you write, as long as it stirs the readers curiosity, draws the reader in, and creates a lasting impression. Then, by the time you make your sales pitch at the end, the story has been embedded in their sub consciousness and will have triggered various impulses to buy.

Cartoons or images are like mini-stories that can convey a quick synopsis or be a good lead in for a story. If the image captures a visitor's attention enough, they will probably scroll down and read the story behind it. So, don't think that this is all about copy. Use everything you can to draw a visitor into the copy that eventually has your sales pitch at the end and a call to action to buy your product.

There is one other way to implement this strategy that does not involve actually selling the product. Instead, it could be a story that creates the right environment for your product or educates the reader for why your products are necessary or expedient. This is particularly effective for items that may be so novel that people don't know why they would buy them. There is no conditioning in place or market buzz that has been associated with the item and so they're left not understanding the value of the product at all.

That's when you need a story about your particular industry and how these products were developed to fulfill a particular need. You want to be clear that people understand the results they will get in their lives by paying attention to this particular issue and this sets the environment for making a sales call at the end.

For example, when organic products first came out, only people who were into health foods understood the reasons for buying higher- priced produce or hormone-free meats. It just didn't have a mass appeal and the consumer wasn't really aware that there really was any difference between meat at the local supermarket and meat that was brought up hormone-free and cost much more. Why would you pay that much more for something that you don't understand or value?

So, it took a while for people to realize that our air and water systems are polluted and that farms use all kinds of chemicals as fertilizers on produce that end up in the vegetables and fruits. So, if you happened to be selling some organic product online, you might have a story on the environmental stresses that cause your products to be necessary for a healthy diet. Once you declare the proper environment and frame the value of your product or service, it becomes much more intriguing and interesting to your potential buyer. So, what might not have been something they saw any value in, becomes very important to try so that they too can see the results in their life.

So, while a story is typically something that can relate the potential buyer to a common experience that will help them bond, there are other times when you have to set the stage first before they get why it is a common experience. It may be they have never ever tried anything organic in their lives, so you had to introduce that concept to them from some other area that is familiar to them—our polluted environment.

Timing this strategy

Telling a story that is brief can be done at the very beginning of a sales encounter. It can be done on the home page, in your about me pages, or when you are introducing a new product. Once you've established a nice bond, you can even get into longer stories on the sales page to establish the benefits of your product, especially if it is something new that needs to have the stage set for it to make a dramatic appearance.

You can even use a "joke of the day" type of device to help engage your readers and have it introduce your industry, if not your product. Sort of like the jokes that all relate to screwing in a light bulb. If you happened to be selling light bulbs, this would make an excellent way to establish rapport and humor on your site and eventually sell light bulbs.

Some people like stories so much that they will email them to other people. You can have an "email this story to your friend" feature that is a great way to have people visiting your market for you. In the same way, a YouTube video that goes viral will work marketing magic for you and you don't have to go and post it to too many places. Other people will start doing it for you.

Most stories will do nothing more than introduce the product or establish rapport. Those are the ones you use on other sites and throughout the Internet to establish a presence online. Reserve the longer, deeper, stories for your website where people can become involved in an area that has calls to action to buy your products.

Flaunt your expertise

People love to deal with experts. Experts can be trusted. Experts are "in the know." And, when we deal with experts, we feel smart for being able to spot them. So, when you want people to automatically give you more credibility and authority to encourage them to do business with you more, flaunt your expertise.

That's right, no one else is going to do it for you and this is something that is not only all right, on the Internet, but it is easily done. It's called self-promotion and the Internet makes it a very easy thing to do online. If you want people to recognize you for your expertise, you will want to concentrate on your area of expertise and then show off what you know. It's that simple.

The strategic plan

There is a fine line between coming off as an expert and being a pretentious imposter or know-it-all. If you really don't know what you're talking about, that is going to come across sooner or later. So, you do want to know your market niche extremely well. You should do enough research so that you can even anticipate your customers concerns and have solutions ready for them when they come up. You will want to be the person who not only knows your market, but the desires of your customers too. Then, you will want to visit places that can allow you to show off that knowledge without seeming pretentious or an attention hog. Least of all, you don't want to visit just to spam a group with your expertise when it's not even related to the discussion. You should pick the venues that you will be using to show off your expertise very carefully. They should include forums, discussion groups, blogs, your website, and sales page that allow you to add information that gathers attention and solves a problem without it appearing to be a direct solicitation.

This means that you will need to spend some time creating your online image as the expert in residence. You will have to write articles, author eBooks, write in other people's blogs, do guest posts, frequent discussion groups, enter topics into forums, and more. It's not easy being an expert, but it's well worth it.

Some people build their image as an expert by collecting titles or degrees. That's perfectly legitimate. If you have a PhD, flaunt it. Put the initials after you name in all your email correspondence and on your website too. There's nothing wrong with having extra initials after your name and you'd be surprised the air of credibility and authority that this gives you.

Use any advantage you have to express your authority on a subject. If you are selling clothing, for instance, you don't want images on your website that show people dressed in frumpy attire. If you are trying to sell office supplies, you don't want people on the site photographed in shorts and sandals. This type of subtle visual statement leads people to question your expertise, not because you yourself are portrayed less professionally, but because you don't associate with people who have authority. People with power generally congregate with other people with power.

If you show up with less-than-ideal business partners or affiliates, your expertise and authority are questioned, not to mention your judgment.

The psychological triggers

Since we were children, we have been taught to respect authority. We idolized our parents for knowing more than we did and we trusted them to guide us to make the right decisions in life. Later, in school, we are put into an educational system that grades us based on our knowledge of the course material with the teachers being the ultimate symbol of someone with the most expertise in a subject. They were the ones we were supposed to respect and listen to. After we started work, the same rules apply.

Those people who know the system or the game of politics, the experts in the company who deal with the other experts, are the ones that demand our respect and obedience. Through them, we gain our promotions and get the good things in life.

This habit of obedience to authority and recognition of experts as the final say in life never really goes away. It's been impressed upon us since early childhood and, in many cases, a trusted expert becomes the reflection of a trusted parent. We are more inclined to listen to these experts, even feeling a sense of gratitude that there is someone to listen to who can guide us in the proper choices to make. It makes our lives easier, and it becomes a subconscious desire to follow authority just as we've been programmed to do. It is so ingrained that some people never question an expert, even if it appears they may not be all that trustworthy. They are so accustomed to having someone to tell them what to do that they actually can feel very reassured just by having someone willing to take up the mantle of authority for them.

Since marketers know that showing your expertise is a great way to make a sale, there is plenty of competition from people trying to sell themselves as experts. It's up to you to differentiate your own knowledge, image, and authority from everyone else so that people are more likely to come to you than the next guy.

How to implement effectively

To become an expert on the web is easy. All you have to do is make sure people know your qualifications and be careful to always project the image of an expert everywhere you go. Unlike a job interview that requires someone who you worked with to offer a reference, you can be your own reference on the web. For that, you want to take the time to develop this strategy everywhere, not just for yourself, but your company image too.

As we mentioned earlier, you will want to mine your personal experience and express that whenever appropriate.

If you have a Master's or a PhD, be sure to use those initials after your name when you email, when you add a post to a discussion group or forum, or even when you comment on a blog. It's a very simple matter and it adds loads of authority to your current image. When people see those initials, they will be triggered to defer to you automatically. So, be sure to put ALL initials that represent some degree of expertise next to your name.

If you are doing this for your website or business image, you want to capture your expertise in a single phrase that represent why people should do business with you. This can be like "voted best value for the money by Consumer Magazine." Of course, only add that if it's true!

You don't want to be caught echoing some claim that later points out that you clearly don't have any expertise and are a liar to boot! So, be genuine, but also be sure to take pride in your accomplishments. If you don't have any recognition from others that you can point to, you can still raise the audience's awareness of what makes your business special. Maybe you are the biggest distributor on the East Coast for your particular item. Maybe you make the most unique ukuleles in Hawaii. Maybe you are the oldest company on record for the business.

Believe it or not, people hold a great deal of respect for businesses that can say they've been around for decades. Imagine if you could say that about your online business where most have a habit of disappearing overnight? It creates the image of tremendous stability and also expertise in your area of commerce.

If you still can't think of anything, start by telling your audience why you think your business or staff is special. Maybe you think you have the best group of positive thinkers on staff who find ways to make everyone's day brighter.

Maybe you sell environmentally friendly profits and for each sale you donate to a green cause. This can make people think that you know about the issues important to them and they can trust you as an expert because you walk your talk.

So, ask yourself a few questions to help you establish what makes you or your business experts on your market niche:

- What credentials do I have to prove our expertise?
- Are my workers specially trained or gifted?
- How many years have you been in business?
- What is your satisfaction rating for customers?
- What separates your knowledge from your competitors?
- What image should you be portraying to be considered an expert?
- Am I or my company certified by any outside agencies?
- Who else thinks you or your business is expert in your market niche?
- What do I know that no one else knows?

Once you have the answer to those questions, you can write up articles and feed them to article directories. At the end, in your author's bio box, you can add information on who you are and your status as an expert. Either submit the articles to directories yourself or hire a company to do it for you. These article directories will show up in search engines when someone searches for your company name or your own name. If you have multiple different articles out there under different directories, the search results on a search engine will bring up so many results that you look like an instant expert!

That's one way to get your name out there as an expert fairly quickly. Another way is to visit forums and discussion groups that are within your target niche. Add to the discussions, when you can show off your knowledge and increase your exposure online. If you keep coming back and doing this, at least that audience will begin to equate your name or your company's name as experts in a particular field. And, that also will show up in search results from a search engine.

Writing a book and putting it up on Amazon or some other large distributor will also qualify you as an expert. It used to be that you had to find a publisher to publish your book to really be perceived a formally approved expert. That's not the case anymore. Anyone can self-publish a book and then submit it to online retailers for sale. You can even do an eBook format and offer it for free in various places and build your reputation that way too. Just make sure your books contain reference to your website, your products, and your own credentials.

Finally, you can ask to do guest posts to other people's websites or solicit testimonials for your own website and products. Guest posts on big blogs are particularly effective because it builds traffic as well as allows you to target your particular niche and convert it to sales. And, major bloggers are always looking for guest posters from noted experts so that they can take a break every now and then from posting.

If you are on Facebook, the number and quality of friends and social network that you build can add to your reputation as an expert. If you have a network of 300 people who all are big names in your industry, which automatically qualifies you as a big name too. Its authority and expertise solely by association.

Timing this strategy

The time to self-promote is ALWAYS. It can't be said enough. You might get tired of constantly re-iterating the same catch phrases that note your expertise, but you don't know what new prospects are coming in that will need that reassurance. You want to do it when you are at other people's sites, when you are not selling but rather building a marketing presence online, and when you are selling too.

Almost every interaction you have should echo your expertise so as to trigger that deep-seated desire to obey the call to action later. You don't want to come off as demanding, but simply showing you know your stuff and that they can have a quiet confidence in your history, knowledge, or products can be a great way to trigger the desire to buy.

Prove the product's true worth

In online marketing, you want to get rid of any fears the buyer may have over purchasing your products or services. People have a big fear of being taken advantage of or buying something that later makes them feel like a fool for being duped into the purchase. There are other people who are always looking for a good deal and demand that they get a high return on their financial investment, no matter what they're buying.

Since you are dealing with consumers who are Internet savvy, you know that they will be able to compare your products or service easily simply by browsing other companies online or doing a quick search through Google. So, you will have to beat them to that and provide whatever comparisons they need to prove your product's true worth. It's far better for you to do it, and limit and frame the results of your research to make your product appear favorably. Then it is for them to do it and figure out that there is at least one product out there that is a better deal for them or has some feature they like better.

This is particularly important if your product has no brand name. Maybe you are selling your own line of products and competing against much better-known brands. If you cannot prove your product's true worth in a relatively short amount of time, there's no reason for a sales prospect to even consider buying your product. The fear of being taken will override the possibility of getting a good deal. So, again, you have to make sure they know they are getting just as good a value as the name brands you are competing against, or maybe even a better value.

The strategic plan

When you are targeting value as your main selling point, you want to be able to educate your potential buyer not just about your products, but about the overall market offerings too. So, that means, you have to do a little more research than just being aware of your own value, as compared to other products in your own inventory. Instead, you want to be aware of the product's value when compared to the rest of the market that the sales prospect will eventually want to view.

There are two factors involved here: quality versus price. Price is often not the determining factor for buying a product, unless that product is being compared to the same product somewhere else for a lower price. So, if you have a top selling product available in your inventory, price will determine how good a value someone perceives it to be. Now, however, if you are working with a range of products, and not a specific brand, then you want to concentrate on quality, more than price. The more features, the higher the quality, than the competition and the product becomes a better value, regardless of the price. This may seem odd, but that's because the actual intrinsic value of the product is more, when compared to the rest of the other products on the market.

The psychological triggers

When people see you comparing your own products and are educated about the product's intrinsic value, they equate a better value with a lower price, even if your price is actually much higher than your competition. In other words, it's like a unit price at the grocery store. When people go to compare two different cans of peaches at the store, they look at all the canned peaches and decided which they want to buy. If they are focused solely on price, they will look for the generic brands and not even bother looking at the different types of peach syrups or even the weight by can. Instead, they will gravitate to cheaper brands because that's what they're looking for to start: a deal on the price. Value is not a consideration until after that when they will look at the unit price for that brand to determine which can actually is the better deal by weight. That's when price is a consideration for value only.

However, most people don't buy items this way. They want to go and shop and come home with something they are proud of and feel they got a great deal on too. For that, they would be the buyer that goes to the grocery store and looks at all the canned peaches. They look at the labels and they admire the different ways the peaches are sliced or diced. They look at the types of syrups, light or heavy. They look to see if any are special peaches for some reason.

So, what they are comparing is the value based on the characteristics and features of each brand. Then, when they find a couple of brands they like, they start to look at unit prices. In their mind, the fact that the value is so much higher in one brand than another automatically reduces the expense of them, and that's the first priority. After that price may be a consideration, but let's face it, they will be higher than the generic prices. It's just that the cheaper peaches are simply not worth their money, in their perception.

So, when you are going to show your product's intrinsic value it's important to highlight the features that make it special. If you are comparing it to name brands, you have to show why your product is a better value, not based solely on price, but on the features that it offers or the quality of the product. Otherwise, very few people are willing to spend their money on cheap products just to save a few bucks. They know that after a bit of time, the cheap products break and they will just have to go out and get a new product much more quickly.

How to implement effectively

This is probably the most complicated strategy to implement. It requires you to take the time to educate your sales prospect in a way that they find informative and enlightening, instead of boring. You can do this quickly with a table of comparison with check marks for features, and that tool works very well here. However, what happens when you have features that your customer won't even understand? That's truly the case when you are dealing with technical equipment and people really don't know whether one processor is really better than another. That's when you also have to educate them on why they want that feature too.

That's why you will want to be a little more descriptive here than normal. It can be a bit of a drain for people coming to your site to find a long list of features, but it will be necessary to educate the buyer. You can have the short summary in a table and then a bulleted list underneath to indicate what each feature is all about. That way, when someone comes to your website who is knowledgeable on your products, they won't bother to read the bulleted list. The table of comparison is sufficient. Those that don't have that same background will read the list and be impressed that you took the time to educate them on the features and why they are important to them. It shows that you care enough to make them informed consumers.

Another way you can implement this strategy is to have a short story that talks about why the features on your product are a good value. Maybe you are selling purses and your purses are leather and not synthetic. Maybe they have features like a cell phone compartment, an accompanying wallet that matches, and the potential to add your personalize monograph too. When you compare your purse to other purses, you will want to show that the reason these things are important is because they serve a function, they help you to express your identity, and they are durable, valuable, or aesthetically pleasing—even more so than your competitor's purses.

You can even bring up the product's price and compare that to show that even though your products cost more, they are a better value. Or you can show that your products cost less and deliver the same or better value! People still want to know that they are saving money, whether it is through quality or price value.

One way to help you get higher sales is to offer the cheaper product first. The way this works is that people will be so excited by the low price on the cheaper product that when you bring out the higher priced version of that product, they will transfer their excitement to the new product and equate it as a better value. Most of the time, when they hear about all the additional features they get for just x amount of dollars more, they will jump at the chance of getting an even bigger value than they thought they were getting with the cheaper version.

This strategy of offering several versions works well when you are comparing items too. You don't want to compare apples to oranges, so several different versions of the same product in your inventory greatly increase your potential for making a sale. After all, you are giving the customer a choice, it just so happens the choice is still going to mean a sale for you. So, it doesn't matter how you compare them or what features they have, the fact that they are able to figure out for themselves whether it really is price or intrinsic value that will motivate them to buy helps you to make a sale.

This strategy can be turned on its head to still offer a sales opportunity, particularly if you are selling memberships or fundraising for an online charity. In that case, you would not offer the cheapest alternative first. You would show them the most expensive option first. When people balk at that, you would then offer the cheaper alternative. The reason for that is that they are not so much comparing products, but services or donations. When they buy, they're not going to get anything placed in their hands, unless of course you make that an option for the higher priced memberships.

If you are selling packages, like trips to other countries that include hotel, airfare, and sightseeing, you should start with the highest priced package first. Packages include many different benefits and will automatically be perceived to have a higher value than a single item. So, you don't want to start with the cheaper package in this instance. Then, you can offer the cheaper products as an alternative if the higher priced package is rejected.

So, when you are considering implementing this strategy think about the order you want to present your products online. Do you want to highlight the higher priced item first and then offer the lower one or vice versa? You could try it both ways and then see when you make more sales. That's the answer to your problem then. But, be aware, that the order of product presentation will influence people on subconscious levels in the area of proving your product's value.

Timing this strategy

This strategy can be done when people are browsing your product inventories. When they search your site for a particular product, make sure the other products in that inventory show up too. Depending on what they are looking for you can manipulate the order of display to influence them to perceive a higher value.

If you are competing against brand names and using your own generic products, be sure to include that information on your sales page so people know your products are worth it. If you are writing copy ads that are going in printed material, you can compare your products quickly and then put a link to a site where you sell the product.

You can also educate your customer on getting a better value just before they check out. It's like when you go to a fast-food place and you order a single item. That's the time when you're told that if you buy a combo package you get a better value. And, most people then buy the combo whether they actually were that hungry or not. The same can be done online, by saying on the checkout, "did you know that for x amount more you could get such and such?" If you have that placed as standard programming in your website, then it will come up and alert the customer that there is a potential for a better value deal and usually bigger bucks for you.

Conclusion

As you can see from these strategies, there are ways to influence a customer who is visiting your site to cause them to buy your products. However, you have to understand your audience, your products benefits, and the correct timing as to when to try each strategy. Once you start to implement some of these strategies on your site, you will see that some work better than others on particular products or at different times. If you pay attention to when you go shopping, you can see instances of each of these strategies at work in your own buying behavior. And, many retailers do train their staff to trigger buying behavior by evaluating the consumer's needs and choosing to interact at particular times with particular phrases that trigger the subconscious to buy.

It's really not magic, but it can seem to be at times. People go about their days mostly unconscious of their own motivations and in sales, this can be a big advantage. They may all come from different backgrounds, but still some behaviors like respect for authority, the desire to play with things, and the desire to bond through stories have their start in childhood programming. These daily habits become so powerful that as adults, we don't even think about why we respect experts, what makes something more fascinating than something else, and why everyone loves a good joke! Yet, that is all part and parcel of being human.

Once you begin to understand your own triggers and why you do certain things, it becomes easier to predict what will trigger other people to close a deal or not. They are no different from you and they will follow their better instincts too. So, learn the psychology, seek to understand the dynamics of human behavior, and then try to find ways to influence people to increase your sales. That's how you turn a visitor on your site into a customer and build life-long relationships.

As you get the hang of using all the tools online available to create that hypnotic spell, you will find it easy to flip from forums to blogs to sales pages and maybe even into third-party vendors like eBay. You will build the confidence you need that you know what works and when and what's the appropriate time to use one strategy over another to make a sale. You will have learned that it isn't difficult to engage people online, it just takes a bit more skill since you are not face-to-face with your potential buyers. But, once you have those skills they can be used all over the Internet to help you gather customers and sales from all over the globe.

CHAPTER 4

ULTIMATE TRAFFIC PART II - PROSPECT TO CUSTOMER

Prime the buyer's greed glands

Greed is a human trait, and maybe we'd like to ignore it because it's not very pretty, but it is a fact of life. People do get greedy and when they do, they tend to lose all sense of reason. That's actually a pretty good time to use this human weakness to help you trigger the impulse to buy your products.

In sales, greed isn't just about charging people the most money you can get out of them, although that is definitely one aspect that marketers use. It's also about providing the trigger so that your buyer believes they are getting a steal, either because of a price differential or the cost versus benefits preview. It's a great way not just to make one sale, but to close on a variety of items.

Closeout and bargain hunting are a form of greed even though it's viewed as frugality. It all depends on if the buyer is buying bargains because that's what they practically need in their lives or whether the impulse to buy is spurred more by overactive greed glands that can't turn down anything resembling a steal of a deal. So, placing these types of deals on your website can help you start to develop a sales strategy that attracts a wide range of buyers.

The strategic plan

It may surprise you to know that the disposable income level of your sales prospects actually define what a good deal is, not the actual value of the product or service you are offering. That's because greed is relative to your economic prosperity, even though high income wage earners are not immune to greed, it just takes a slightly different form.

For instance, when you are trying to sell an item that might be worth $60 to a very well-heeled client, you might want to up the price to $100, and highlight the features and quality of the product, and see if they bite. The reason for this isn't just your own greed, but also the understanding that price to value is relative based on your disposable income.

For someone making over $100,000/year, an extra $40 is not seen as a lot of money and they may be used to paying higher prices due to the markets they shop. They might not even question the price. However, they will assuredly question the quality and want to make sure that the purchase reflects their station in life. The greed here is more about status than money.

On the other hand, if you were to do the same with a person making less than $25,000/year that $100 set point may be enough for them to do some comparison shopping and they'll pretty soon find out that they can buy the same item from your competitor for $40 less. You not only lose the sale, but you lose future sales too from that customer. So, using greed to price your products is tricky. You have to understand your target demographic, and specifically the income level of most of your customers. Then, you can price accordingly.

If you are not sure of the income level, you can always start using this strategy by offering a more expensive option first and then presenting a much less expensive option second. The difference in prices and a clear explanation of the differences in features can be enough to make the greed glands in any demographic start to salivate. It appeals to the high income earners because it triggers their status greed in elevating the higher priced item as the "must have" product, not just because of additional features, but precisely because it is more expensive. It triggers the lower end crowd because the less expensive option will be seen to be a minor sacrifice in features for a large reduction in cost.

The psychological triggers

Where does greed come from? It's said it is one of the original seven deadly sins, but it's probably more a survival instinct. When human beings lived at the mercy of the elements and environment, there were wide disparities between times of prosperity and harsh times when drought, famine, or disease might invade the security of the home. So, the instinct to hoard things and try to get a bigger share than someone else, was basically an innate fear of survival because the future was so uncertain.

That's why even people who are very well off are not immune to greed. It is inbred in our species and helped us, as a species, to survive very bad times, albeit at the expense of others at times. But, the instinct to try to get a very good deal, even one you don't need immediately, is something that appeals to everyone, even if the tactic to implement it is different according to your demographic.

In marketing, the skillful manipulation of price is what triggers this dynamic. Value is something that the buyer determines in a capitalistic system, so that it can fluctuate from person to person. So, the way to engage a perception that your product is a steal is by manipulating the price in relation to the perceived value. Let's be clear, the price itself is viewed as a fixed commodity to the buyer, it is the value that is fluctuating from person to person. If the price is low when compared to the perceived value, even if the price is actually quantitatively high, then it is considered a steal by that potential buyer and the greed glands will kick into high gear.

So, you can either raise or lower the price to stimulate greed, it's that simple. That's the tool you have at your disposal. However, always do it in comparison to your understanding of the customer's perceived value of the product.

How to implement effectively

You may be scratching your head a bit confused about raising a price to stimulate greed. There is a strategy that you can use which shifts the perceived value in the buyer's mind while you do it. It is quite a bit more subtle that lowering a price to stimulate greed, but it can be done, especially for luxury or high-priced markets. Remember that as long as the prices are low in comparison to the perceived value, even if it is quantitatively a high dollar value, it's still considered a steal.

Here is how you might try to implement the greed factor in a high- priced market.

Say you are selling collectible fine china. You have several sets that are obviously worth hundreds of dollars and you are interested in getting a stampede of buyers to your door to generate interest in the product. So, you build a marketing campaign and you talk about how the value of the price of this fine china has increased over time substantially and how rare it is becoming. Now, you're attracting the demographics of luxury buyers who are interested in not only quality goods, but they have a nose for great deals too.

So, you say that in another five years, their investment in the fine china may be worth twice as much again. Be careful with the wording and be sure that they understand that past performance of an investment is no guarantee of future returns. So, here we are very skillfully changing the perception of this product from china to collectibles and an investment, not a household purchase, and we've even shown how the value might potentially increase after the purchase. So, are we going to sell it for the actual value of the product? No way! We are selling an appreciating asset, not a household item.

So, now the value of the product has increased tremendously in the buyer's mind and we can command a higher figure than the actual present day value. But, wait! That's just the start of our greed enhancing program. Now, you say, that while it's true that the china is a great investment and of quality and high value, you can offer the public a great deal by offering it at a discount because you are either going out of business, having an end of year sale, celebrating your business anniversary or whatever! Make up an excuse and make it somewhat believable. Then, cut the price of the set from the higher price to a lower one, but one still substantially higher than what the product's present day value is worth.

Another way to do this is not to cut the value of one set, but offer a discount on volume buying. This would work perfectly if you are selling place settings and you don't know whether they want four, eight, or twelve place settings. However, they may think it's too expensive to buy twelve, until you offer them a discount for buying eight or more. You trigger the greed, and they will start to justify the reasons why having extra sets on hand are a good idea.

Finally, lowering the price of items is always a sure-fire way to attract greedy customers by the boat load. And, you will soon discover that the amount of attention and enthusiasm you get for your sales is completely proportional to the difference in price drops. The lower the price, the more you sell, in other words. The only time when you can't make those sales is when the product is obviously junk and no one wants to buy it, but for the most part if you continue to persuade your customers of the innate value of the product and lower the price, you can spur them into action to close the sale.

Timing this strategy

This is a strategy that can be used even before a customer shows up to your website! Yes, that's right, you don't have to wait for them to show interest in your products, you don't have to wait for them to sign up to mailing lists, you can do it as a mass advertising tool to bring customers in who will be attracted by your specials.

This is an excellent tool for people in direct mail and retail sales. You know that when you put out a special in one of those newspaper inserts or ValuPak envelopes, that you are practically guaranteed new customers as long as the offer is enticing enough to convince them to drop by. Well, on the Internet you don't even have to convince them to gas up their cars and make the trip, you can simply put your link out there and invite them to click on it.

You'll want to include your offer in various third-party forums and comment on in discretely where ever you can. Be careful not to spam people, but you do want to advertise it on other places besides your own site.

In order to get the widest exposure, you can offer to give key people in the same niche as you the deal for free, if they review it and write about the value. While that may be a sweet enough deal for some, others will want to get a commission off each product they promote and sell. Then, you can also set up an affiliate program for that special so that they are not only able to promote a great deal to their visitors, but they make money off the deal too. That's the true meaning of greed, when you butter the palms of everyone involved in the deal and make it a win-win-win for everyone.

These types of offers are best as either introductory offers or close- out sales, or end of season sales. There should be a reason why you are able to offer these offers so that people don't become habituated to receiving only sharp discounts from you and get offended when you put up a product at a regular price. And, don't forget the luxury market too when you want to implement this strategy, but instead of money, opt to hype the perceived value so that a lowering of the price still keeps the initial price high.

Impact their emotions

If you think buying is not an emotional experience, you are mistaken! Every word in sales copy is amplified when it triggers an emotional response and can be the difference between copy that excites the imagination of the potential buyer and that which deadens it. When you engage the buyer's imagination they can even begin to imagine what it's like to own the product you are selling and it stirs up the flames of desire for possessing it.

It is true that if you want to sell, you want to sell by impacting the emotions of your potential buyer. Even though you know that the final decision may be justified through logic, the initial way to get by the mind that will think up all sorts of objections to the sale is to appeal to the emotions.

The strategic plan

When you are advertising your products or services you will want to pay close attention to the words you choose. Words are powerful tools on the Internet that you can use to frame the way a person perceives not only the value of your product, but also the experience of possible ownership. Words tell stories that inform your readers about how this product or service solved a problem for some other buyer. Stories can pull a buyer into identifying with the other buyers and help them to visualize their own problems being solved, their lives getting easier or better for having made the purchase.

You will want to pick words that not only tell a vivid story, however, you will also want to use words that influence the buyer's feelings and gives them favorable impressions. It's really not that hard to do. People have a variety of automatic emotional responses to different words. All you have to do is find out which words create the best results and implement them in your sales copy.

You want to create a sales environment that puts people into an emotional mindset. Why? The simple reason is to bypass the logical mind long enough to make the sale. Sure, the final decision to buy will need to be justified with solid benefits, but that's not typically the reason a person ends up making the decision to buy. They may not even be aware that many of their buying decisions are based on how they feel about a product rather than what they think about it. People actually feel thrills when they buy and that thrill acts as a beacon to get them to buy again.

Yet, when they are asked why they buy a particular product, they don't talk about how they feel – that's rather personal! Instead, they list the benefits. That's because when people are asked to justify a purchase, the mind automatically kicks in, even if they made the decision based solely on how they felt at the time of purchase.

The psychological triggers

The brain has two halves and one deals with logic and the other is more intuitive and feeling. The two halves generally don't communicate at the same time in most people. If you have very strong emotions, you're reason is usually blocked from functioning at its highest potential and vice-versa. This can be really useful information in your marketing efforts because if you can get someone to get emotional about your products, you can sell without even really having to work too hard at it.

Not only that, but once an impression is made on the emotional mind, it tends to have a longer memory than the logical mind. It is even well known that feelings can be associated to various stimuli that bring back powerful memories, complete with the emotions, sometimes just by smelling something that reminds you of your childhood. Words aren't just letters strung together that have a logical meaning. They also have a personal meaning. If you can tap into that emotional intelligence and bypass the logical critic most people have standing ready to say no, you will find that you can sell things much faster and retain customers with a higher sense of satisfaction after the sale.

You don't just have to focus on invoking pleasant emotions, because negative emotions can also be powerful motivators to close a sale. Think of people who are in the market to buy GPS systems for their cars. Why would they want to buy that? On an emotional basis, they may be trying to avoid getting lost. So, the feeling you want to invoke is precisely that confused and lost feeling that they dread. And, then offer the GPS system as a solution to never having to feel that way again!

How to implement effectively

The way to implement this strategy is to start making a list of alternative, emotion-packed words that influence your potential buyer in subtle, but powerful, ways. Review your copy for opportunities where you can reach out and literally touch the buyer and comfort or assure them that they are making the right decision to buy.

One word that is very powerful and should be used more in copy is the word "invest" instead of buy. When you buy something it almost has the connotation of being taken for a ride. For instance, when you "buy into" something it means you've been convinced, maybe even despite your feeling it may not be such a good idea. However, the word "invest" has the opposite feeling. It gives you a feeling of security and reaping returns, even if you don't have a logical explanation for why that is so. It's just a good investment.

People in the real estate industry are masters at this game. When a house is small, they call it "cozy." When the walls are painted in odd colors, they call it "custom paint." If it is falling apart at the seams, they call it a "handyman special." These are euphemisms that don't completely hide the meaning, but reframe it to show off the positive aspects of it. They plug into the emotional impact of the words. Cozy gives you the idea of warmth and being hugged by your mother.

Custom paint is a term that can mean anything from a personalized mural complete with the kid's hand prints to a mural vista of the French Riviera by a local artist. It's up to the person reading the ad to fill in the blanks and normally they will fill them in with whatever appeals to them. Handyman special gives you an idea that it's a property that won't last long, being special, and that it only needs little fixes here and there.

So, paying attention to the choice of words is important to implement this strategy. That can be done by pure trial and error or by looking up sales books to find which words carry a positive impact. There are many such words that you see in television ads, like the words "new, improved, easy" and more. Or, you can just start to switch words here and there in your copy and see what impact it makes on your bottom line.

The second way to implement this strategy is to bring out your inner drama queen. You want to be able to exude emotion and have that pour all over your sales copy. Try to write up an offer that really engages someone on an emotional level. Use it in your sales presentations by trying to bring in an emotional content that people can quickly identify with and then use it to manipulate people into a frame of mind that makes them buy.

Especially, you want to focus on framing the benefits in an emotional framework.

This will help your buyer begin to imagine and experience your product more in their feelings. Try to describe the product in emotional language that triggers people into associations that are positive for them. This is the same idea that real estate people use when they advise you to bake cookies or simmer cinnamon sticks in the house before you show it. The scents pull in memories of mom baking in the kitchen and make the sale for you through subconscious emotional associations. Well, you can do the same with words by painting the picture of the emotional trigger for them to be able to visualize it better in their mind.

Obviously, depending on your demographics, the emotional triggers for one group may be different from another. It's your job to figure out which emotional triggers will appeal to the people you are marketing. If you are marketing to hurried, working moms then triggering the image of a crying, babies, and the phone ringing, while dinner burns on the stove, would sell anything that makes this scenario go away. It might be easy to make microwave meals, it can be an answering machine that shows you who is calling and whether it's important. It's not always going to be obvious how to associate the emotion to your product, but it should be relevant to your demographic.

If you were to use that same imagery to try to sell microwave meals for single professionals, they would not relate to it, even if the microwave meal might appeal to them if it had been framed differently. Do you see how the emotion is triggered specifically by the advertising and the target audience? For some, the emotional trigger will strike them right where they live, and for others, it simply leaves them cold. You have to know who you are marketing to, to understand how to trigger the emotions that you want to associate with your advertising copy.

Some emotions are universal because they relate to our childhood. We all equate home with feelings of security (which is good for the real estate market). We all want to feel included and accepted by our family and friends. We all want to feel we are achieving or accomplishing something we can feel proud of. These types of emotions can also be used to mine a larger audience, when you are unsure of your demographics. But, the more targeted your emotional marketing campaign the greater the possibility that it will be a stronger influence to trigger buying behavior.

Timing this strategy

The time to use this strategy is when you are first present-ing the product to the public or your website visitor. Don't wait to start to bring some familiarity to the product that the person can begin to identify with it as the solution to their problems. Try to engage all the senses so that they can begin to tie into the sensual aspect of the product – this will lead to the emotional part of their brain and bring forth associated positive memories. Once that first impression is made in the emotional part of the brain, it will be very hard to shake later on.

That's part of the reason that many expert sales people will actually take a sample with them to a presentation, something their potential buyer can touch and experience. It appeals to the emotional side of all human beings and gets them to start imagining what it would be like to own the regular product all to themselves.

Think of how car manufacturers present their advertis-ing for cars. They typically show a convertible car winding down a stunning coastal highway, sea breeze flying through the driver's hair, as the sun beats down on dazzling water and sand. You can practically smell the salt air and taste the spray of sea water in your mouth, and that's the point. They evoke the emotional response by getting you to imagine buying the car. You then become that person with the perfect life that has the wind wiping through your hair in a breezy, freeing, experience while everyone else is stuck in a cubicle hard at work. It's really quite amusing when we analyze how easily our emotions are manipulated, but that's really the case. There are certain desires that most human beings will do anything to experience: love, freedom, joy, and success. Tie those emotions to your product, and you've got a winner.

Go beyond the 100% satisfaction guarantee

Everyone remembers the cheesy 100% satisfaction guarantee that old television infomercials would haul out to get people to believe in their products. Well, consumers are much more savvy now and most people understand this to be more of a trial guarantee that after a certain period expires. In other words, the 100% satisfaction guarantee was usually limited to a few weeks or less, and after that you were stuck with the product. So, in all fairness it was more like a free trial than a 100% satisfaction guarantee. After all, if you're not satisfied and the period for returns has ended, aren't you then still a dissatisfied customer?

So, we're going to tell you how to put in place something that goes beyond the 100% satisfaction guarantee, even though it may seem impossible. Well, it isn't. It is your conviction that the products you offer are of such worth that you can offer a guarantee that goes beyond everyone's expectations and still make money on the product. And, when you have that sort of conviction about the products you sell, the customer begins to believe it too.

The strategic plan

The strategy, on the surface, seems a bit crazy for a business person to implement. What you will suggest to your customers is that if a certain condition is met that you will refund their money or make amends beyond what is expected of you. That means that if you sell a product and it breaks, you promise to refund the money or replace it, even if it's one year or two years down the line.

But, it doesn't just have to be about things breaking, it can also be a usage condition. Say, you buy a subscription to use a particular service and then find you don't use it enough to pay for the membership costs. In this strategy, the way to go beyond the 100% satisfaction guarantee is to offer to refund all the money for the subscription if you don't use the products and services offered by the membership at all within the year. Of course, you would have to have a way of figuring that out.

In a discount club, you have membership costs that give you access to discounts on other products. The idea is that the amount of money you save will easily exceed the membership cost to sign up and you eventually make back your membership fee. But, what if you didn't do that? Would most companies offer you the membership fee back if you found that the use of the club wasn't worth it? Well, if your membership club did this it would set itself above the rest by offering to ensure that whether a member uses the membership they bought or not, they will end up satisfied with the purchase because you will make sure to go beyond the typical business guarantee. Now, add a little perk at the end like a free gift or even a coupon for monies off popular items for having just tried the membership, even if it didn't end up saving you money, and people will flock to sign up.

The psychological triggers

There are lots of people who offer guarantees, but they are only worth the person issuing them. Many times there are clauses in the guarantee that limit the actual worth, such a specific limited time period or meeting a specific condition that is unlikely to happen.

For instance, most tires these days are sold with six year or 60,000 mile warranties. That's a guarantee that should your tire fail before then, it will be replaced for free, right? Wrong! If you look at the fine print, it says that they will replace your tires if the problem is a defect in the workmanship, not for any unforeseen event that might cause your tire fails. Your tires can hit a nail in the road – a far more likely event – and you will have to still pay to replace the tire. And, should your tire fail out of poor workmanship it's still up to you to prove that's the case, instead of it being because somebody slashed your tires or some other environmental danger hit it. It's just not very likely you'll ever use a warranty these days for tires on a manufacturer defect because most tires are made pretty well these days, no matter what they cost.

However, tires are sold based on these guarantees as if the extra money you pay for a really good tire with an excellent warranty is going to give you additional customer satisfaction and security. It really isn't. It's the 100% money back guarantee that really isn't about satisfaction as much as it is about clever marketing, and people realize that.

However, when people are willing to put their money where their mouth is, and put it in writing, that is a very impressive act that creates instant credibility. That means that you will replace or make good on any product, regardless of the reason, no matter what happened or how long it took to occur. Isn't that positively crazy these days? Maybe so, but it also means that you believe above 100% in your company and in its ability to meet the customer's needs. You are betting that your product is so good that people won't need to return it, and that's what you're saying with the beyond 100% satisfaction guarantee.

The person viewing the ad thinks that you are either crazy to make such a good offer or your product is really all you say it is! Otherwise, how could you afford to make this type of guarantee? It raises the perceived value of your product or service and instills confidence in the purchase decision. People know that when they see that over 100% satisfaction guarantee that the likelihood of being taken is very small, and that triggers their confidence in making the purchase. Because you believed in your products, they fell in line and believed in them too. It removes any remaining doubts or resistance to buying the product that a customer might hold in their minds.

How to implement effectively

Implementing this strategy is very easy, it just takes guts. After all, you are basically saying you are willing to show customers that you mean business and that your word can be trusted. If you issue a claim that goes beyond the 100% satisfaction guarantee, you had better be able to back it with action. If you issue it and then go back on your word, you will have a publicity nightmare on your hands and the backlash will be tremendous. So, whatever you promise, be sure you can deliver it and then stick to your word.

This strategy shouldn't be implemented as a standalone strategy. It should always be used as an additional boost to get the customer over the sales finish line. It might be well used for products where there might be some doubts lingering in the minds of the buyer, either because of the price or the novelty. Maybe you are selling a new technology that is designed to do something really novel, but people don't know how helpful it's really going to be. They may read the benefits and even be considering it but the product still needs an additional push to make the customer decide to shell out big bucks to try it. Then, you would trot out the beyond 100% satisfaction guarantee and now those people on the fence will rush to buy.

If you think that you will end up losing too much money refunding purchases or replacing products, you are not realizing that most buyers have short memories. Maybe they buy that high tech air cleaning and filtering system from your store only because they're told if it ever breaks, they can return it for a free replacement. But, odds are when it does break they won't even remember what store they bought it from, much less than you offered them that guarantee.

If they do remember, they might think they need the box or the receipt in order to take advantage of the guarantee, and that might or might not be the case. And, then after that, they have to motivate themselves to get back to your store and try to take you up on that beyond 100% guarantee with the product in hand. Most people will simply go out and buy something to replace the broken product and not even think about your offer again.

It's a sad statement on the American consume mind, but most people are not as frugal or careful with their purchases to document the guarantees and keep track of them. It may be a real factor when they are trying to make the decision to buy, but after that it's mostly forgotten unless that guarantee is such a classic aspect of your marketing that you make it over and over again to multiple customers. Then, you will find that people begin to associate that product or your company with that guarantee and they will take you up on it more, but still not at a high rate.

Let's be clear, you aren't just going to offer a good guarantee, you are offering an UNBELIEVABLE guarantee. It's so good, people will think you're nuts for offering it. They may just buy the product to try and prove you wrong. If you are selling subscriptions to a discount club, they might be so intrigued by your offer, and knowing they have nothing to lose, and even maybe something to gain, they will put their money down and see if you are right.

The UNBELIEVABLE part should come when you're not only offer to keep them from losing money on the deal, but also add some incentive to sweeten the deal should the product not meet their expectations. So, for a subscription to a discount club, you offer to give them a free gift at the end of the year AND their money back just for trying the membership, if they find that they don't make up all the money in discounts throughout the year that they paid in the membership fee. What this tells people is that you believe that EVERYONE will save money using your discount club because you're just that fantastic. You're so convinced that's the case, which you're even willing to pay people to try your club out and offer them a free gift should that not occur as you expect.

To figure out which offers need this additional strategy, you should look at your sales numbers. Are some offers languishing while others are going gang busters? Don't fix what isn't broken. Instead, opt for the slow movers to try this strategy as an additional incentive to move those other offers into better performance.

This is definitely a trial and error business when deciding which offers need it and which don't. If you find that after implementing the beyond 100% satisfaction guarantee, your sales jump 200%, then you know that you've got it in the right place. That's the power this strategy has when you use it with offers that may need just that extra boost to get them to go from underperformers to star sellers.

Timing this strategy

Since this is not a standalone strategy, you want to choose other strategies to pull out first. Then, after you have made the case for your product, through selling the benefits, and you notice that you still have the customer teetering on the seat of their chairs biting their nails over the decision, then try the beyond 100% satisfaction guarantee at the very end of the copy. That's right. We want it at the very end of all the selling copy. You may think that's the worst place for it, but it's really the only place for it.

That's because if a person has gotten that far down the sales page and still hasn't made up their mind, then you need to add something to push them over the edge. If you did it earlier, you would not have a chance to implement the other strategies that can help you make the sale instantly. This one works best when there is still some doubt left in the mind of the potential buyer that needs to be removed, and therefore it goes last.

Walk the logic labyrinth

While an emotional trigger will help to stimulate buying behavior, when it comes time to justify the purchase buyers often seek out logic. No one likes to feel that they've been taken on a deal, and so the end result that even if the emotions have carried them away, they will always give a logical reason why they eventually bought the product. That's because people don't admit that it was an emotional response that instigated the buy, they'd rather admit there was a valid reason for the purchase.

Knowing this, that a logical reason may be necessary for some to close a deal, then you want to provide that logical reason just as you would attempt to resolve an objection before it is raised. It doesn't mean that the reason has to really make any sense, it just has to be enough to justify the purchase. It has to answer the question: "Why should I buy this product?"

The strategic plan

Here you are going to aim a very definite reason why a customer should buy your product. It's typically done after an emotional appeal, to seal the deal and give your ad a double whammy. You are going to look at the demographics of your visitors and you are going to try to put yourself in their shoes. What would be the defining reason to buy this product?

There are a variety of reasons that can trigger different segments of the population to agree that to purchase your product makes sense. If you are dealing with people who are budget conscious, you can go after economic reasons. Another possibility is to focus on health as a reason. Maybe they are getting older and more health conscious. Maybe you are selling something to people who are sick. That can be a powerful reason to consider buying your product. Safety is also something is top-most in people's minds. This might work well for some people and not for others. Safety means different things to different people. For mothers, child safety might be the reason that you need to express to close the deal. For elderly people, it might be personal safety when they are home alone.

Aside from very logical reasons like that, you don't have to just concentrate on those. Sometimes some of the best reasons are status, especially if you are selling in the luxury market. In that case, the reason you give might be, "You deserve it!" Is there any logic to that? Not from an intellectual perspective, but from a reasoning standpoint it makes perfect sense to a certain subset of people, particularly the affluent.

Another reason that you can use is that it will enhance your personal or professional recognition. That can be a powerful reason for people who are dating or seeking some sort of career advancement. Again, the reason you choose should fit the demographic of people you are marketing to.

The way this strategy works best is if you can get into the mindset of the people you are marketing to and understand what type of objections they are likely to raise for themselves. If you are not sure what they are, you need to do a little market research with similar products that are selling online. Without understanding some of the potential objections that people might be thinking about when they view your sales page, you will not be able to successfully resolve them in a logical manner, and that's the key to this strategy.

Once you determine the most typical objections, you will be able to think up the proper justifications to overcome them. By doing so, you will eliminate the last bit of resistance in your buyer's mind and close the sale.

The psychological triggers

Our Western culture prides itself on being one of reason and logic. We rely on our intellectual capabilities to justify almost every aspect of our very existence. Since we are young, we are told that civilized people use reason and not emotion to understand their world. While that remains a deep part of our conditioning, the truth is that we react emotionally first and then we attempt to justify our emotions with our thinking minds.

So, when the emotion is felt to make a purchase, we question it.

We have a certain suspicion about salesmen and slick marketing tactics. The emotion stirred up by the copy may be so strong that people are just waiting to find the reason to justify to themselves that, yes indeed, this is a really good purchase. But, without that reason, the sale is not finalized. That's because our conditioning steps is to warn us that anything that seems too good to be true, usually is unless we rationally analyze our course of action.

A good salesman anticipates that as the starting point of a sale's negotiation, not the end. He or she understands that the person who begins to create objections in their mind is actually considering buying the product, but the mental conditioning and inherent distrust built up about deals may be causing them to hesitate. The way they are taught to hesitate is to analyze the situation with their minds. So, those people that are raising objections are already half- sold! Otherwise, they'd simply walk away and never engage in any thought process to defend themselves from a potentially making a poor decision. It's your job, as an online marketer, to understand what objections are typically going to occur at this stage of the game, and resolve them satisfactorily to reduce the resistance to your sale.

How to implement effectively

One can get very creative in implementing this strategy because the mind has a way of creating excuses when it really wants something. Realize that the sale was probably already made on an emotional basis, all you are doing now is closing the sale by engaging the proper reason to assuage our cultural conditioning. So, even though you can go after reasons that make sense and go along with the product, there are plenty of reasons that don't exactly have to tie into the product, but offer some benefit and can be used to walk the logic labyrinth.

For instance, say you are leasing vehicles. Well, you can talk all day long about the wonderful qualities of the vehicles and how leasing is such a flexible option. But, the final reason that may make the most sense from a business perspective may be the potential ability to write off the lease on the company's taxes. You may wonder, where did that come from? Well, if you understood the demographic that is buying your product most, you may discover that it is companies that are leasing vehicles so they don't have to buy their own and maintain them. Instead, they buy a lease and use them only when they are under warranty. Maybe they even have a specific brand that fits their needs best and are already sold on that one model. So, then, you know that other companies who are in competition may not understand how they save by leasing a vehicle, instead of buying. So, that can be a powerful logical argument to overcome objections from new customers who never thought about leasing before.

In this scenario, the reason actually had very little to do with the product's features or quality. It had to do with a competitive edge and the ability to rationalize the purchase as a smart business expense. So, that's how you can get extremely creative with this particular strategy. Don't just limit your reasons to things that tie into the product, but widen your net and cast it into the biggest possible incentive that makes sense for your demographic.

However, if you find that you need to go with standard reasons, there are always reasons available tied to any product. For instance, if you sell clothing, you may want to iterate how practical it is, how it can be thrown in the washer, or even how classic it is that you can mix and match it with many different styles. Whatever you choose, it has to be something of interest to your demographic.

If you are selling technology, you can focus on how it does a specific function better than other products, how it can improve your productivity, how it simplifies a particular task. These are all very logical reasons that appeal to that crowd.

One thing to remember when implementing this strategy is that it is related to the price you set for your product. In other words, if you have a high priced item, you will have to justify it more than a less expensive product. The only time that may not be true is when you are marketing to an affluent demographic. Otherwise, you will always have to justify a more expensive product to someone, even if they are head over heels in love with it.

Take for instance, luxury cars. There's really nothing all that much different from the way one car operates over another. So, they have to be sold on the features and the reasoning they give is that even though it may have the same parts as another car, they are somehow better quality. It may be a car known for its smooth ride, or it may be known for its high safety record, whatever the reason, it's really something that suggests the car outperforms other cars. After all, luxury cars are truly expensive. How would anyone be able to justify ever buying one based on the fact that they needed a car that took them from one place to another? Obviously, that strategy would not work!

Instead, the logic has to include why it is so much better than other cars to justify the high cost. Despite this, it's almost certain that people who buy luxury cars are buying them based on the emotional impact. The feeling of specialness, the luxury of owning one, the way it associates them with a specific class of people is what really sells these cars. But, if you were to ask anyone why they bought a luxury car, they would most likely opt to tell you it outperforms other cars because they have to justify the expense to you and to themselves too.

The funny thing about the way to implement this strategy that it can actually pay to put in technical reasons to sell the product, even if most people have no idea what most of the features are in technical language. Take a look at how personal computers are sold. They will tell you it had this much RAM, hard drive space, and all kinds of technical features that the majority of people don't understand. The higher the price, the more the technical features are listed in one long list. That's because they are the reasons that people will justify buying a higher priced computer versus a less expensive one, even if they haven't a clue what all those extra features are all about. They only know they have a very smart computer, and likewise, they feel smart opting for a fully loaded personal computer, even if all they want to do is type up a few emails or letters every now and then.

Timing this strategy

The time to implement this strategy is after you've made the emotional sales pitch and the customer is wavering. It almost always comes at the end of a sales presentation, on the side of the box of the software or as an inset for the PC advertisement. It's not the sole reason anyone is expected to agree to buy your product, it's simply put there at the end to remove the last vestiges of resistance to buying the product.

So, for online marketing, it does go in your list of benefits if you have multiple reasons, but you should have one big reason at the end why this is the very best thing a person can do to resolve the problem that led them to your sales page. You can even put it in as an afterthought, as in, "Don't forget, this product does this and this and you should take advantage of that."

Spur their passion for collecting

Everyone associates collecting with antiques and other niche markets. But, the truth is that every market can use the dynamics of the desire to amass collections of things to spur sales. If you don't believe that then you weren't around when the Beanie Babies craze hit the public. Who on earth would have believed grown adults would run around collecting little creatures made of stuffed bean bags? It became a national craze and those little buggers weren't cheap!

The moral of the story there is that if a manufacturer can create a collecting demand for a product that serves no useful purpose, had a unique and sometimes odd look about them, and you can't even eat or invest it, then how much more can you spur the passion for collecting for items that even have additional reasons to buy? Obviously, collecting isn't just for Beanie Babies or antiques, it's for everything and everyone.

The strategic plan

So, even if you are selling bumper stickers or watches, it doesn't matter. You can use this strategy to increase your sales. Don't believe that just because one person has bought one model, it doesn't mean they may not be interested in other models. In fact, people who buy watches, for instance, will often buy several models and collect them for different occasions. Maybe they want a dress watch for when they are at a classy occasions. Maybe they want a fun and flirty one for parties and another more professional-looking one for the office. You can sell them all three! Isn't that a great way to boost your sales?

So, the thing you want to do for this strategy is to target your existing customers. That's right, this is a strategy that is going to bring out the collecting bug in those people that have already shown an interest in your products. In order to get people to start collecting them, you need to start highlighting the collectible nature of your product. Why would someone want to collect them? Who else is collecting them? Can you display them on a shelf? Are they great to own various styles? What are the benefits of collecting your products?

If you ever watch QVC, you will see the way they tout many of their items as collectibles. They will take a call and the person on the other line will tell them how much they love the product and that they've bought several different models! Then, they start listing either their pride in owning such a great collection and how it good it makes them feel, or they start listing all the reasons for why owning many makes sense.

The psychological triggers

You would think that the act of collecting is stimulated because of greed, but it isn't. Collecting falls into its own psychological niche whereby the collector receives a great deal of pleasure and pride from owning many different models of a particular item. It's not because they are unconsciously trying to save up for poor economic times, as in greed, because even things that have no intrinsic function are collected and enjoyed by many people. So, why do people collect things that may not even have any utility in their lives?

If you've ever collected pennies as a youngster, you know that collecting gives one a sense of achievement. Every new penny you find and fit into its pouch gives you pleasure and a feeling of achievement. When the entire collection is done, you can also show that collection off to your friends for them to admire your achievement as well.

In some cases, the history or uniqueness of the collection can also be a source of great pleasure for collectors. That's why people sometimes collect salt shakers in various styles, not necessarily because they need more than one set of salt shakers in their home. Instead, the uniqueness and variety of the pieces bring out great pleasure in the collector who becomes fascinated by each new variation they can add to their collection.

The emotional investment in the collection grows as the collection grows. It becomes a bigger part of the collector's life and may even get a prominent position of display in the home. It becomes a large source of pride. And, once that addiction sets in the collector may not be able to help themselves and be purchasing new items that are far more expensive than when they first started, just to round out their collection. By that time, you almost don't even have to have a reason to sell a collector on a particular piece if the emotional impact of the piece screams out to them "must have!" And, that's the type of enthusiasm and excitement you want associated with your products because it will lead to residual sales that you can count on.

How to implement effectively

It's funny, but this strategy takes a little setup to implement. If you think about it, why did you get into collecting pennies when you were a kid? Would you have done it if they didn't sell those neat little sleeves with all the dates on each slot that you needed to collect to have the complete collection? So, part of implementing this strategy is to simply offer a display case that people can use to track which items they still need to buy to complete their collection and to give a little history of the entire collection.

You can even offer limited quantities of a specific product and increase the collectible status. That way you can even start by charging more for that product, because it is a limited edition. This is one way to manipulate the perceived value while not really changing the intrinsic value due to the collecting strategy.

Always remember to place the bug in your customer's ears that this is a collectible item. You can send them a display case for free with the purchase of more than one item in the collection. You can highlight how other collections you've offered in the past have increased in value in the secondary market. This will give the idea to your customers that they are buying something that will increase in worth and it becomes "an investment."

Remember that what you are trying to build is excitement about each new model, by helping people keep track of what's out there and when a new one comes along. So, giving each model its own unique identity will also stir up interest in collecting different models. This also helps people who may start to push the craze forward when they buy in volume to resell, particularly if you happen to hit a fad. Then, you can expect your collectibles to fly off the shelf like Beanie Babies.

It also doesn't matter if your product is old and outdated, if you are dealing with people who are collectors. If you remember the example of the old TRS-80 computers, many people now collect them as a vintage item. Sometimes even the fact that something is old adds to its collectors appeal, as it becomes harder to find in our throwaway culture. This is why antiques appreciate in value, even though they may not be intrinsically valuable. Old glass bottles or teddy bears are excellent collectibles just for this reason. Bottles break and teddy bears rarely survive childhood. Those that do then become one of the few vintage of examples of that time period and they are sought after by collectors for just that very reason.

Even things with utility can become collectibles with the right framework, due to the uniqueness of each individual item. For instance, when phone cards came out, they each had their own unique designs. After you used the minutes on the card, some people still liked the designs, so they collected them. However, as with anything that is used and collectible, the new, still packaged, and unused item is worth more! That's why even if a person is buying something that has a utility, they may not necessarily even use it if they are collecting it. Think about what a boon it was for those phone companies to sell phone cards that had minutes that were never used! They sold a product with an intrinsic value in minutes that evaporated because people didn't want to ruin the value of the cards. Instead they kept them in the package and sold them as a collectible design and memorabilia.

But, even things that you may not consider to be highly collectible can be collected by somebody. For instance, old tools may seem like they are beyond their appeal, but gardeners may love the idea of having some vintage tools for display in their gardens as a historic and novel motif.

Once you know you have a person who collects one of your items, you know that you have a potential to get them to collect other types of items you sell. For instance, if you find a subset of your customers collecting your watches, maybe they'd also like to collect cuff links. Or if you can find a way to associate another collectible with the first, then you can start cross selling those items. For instance, maybe you have someone who is collecting toy trains. Well, how many other toys do you have that are whimsical and cute enough to be collected? How about all the accessories that you can sell to toy train collectors? Don't they need little mini depots? How about different cabooses? How about books on the history of toy trains or the actual steam engines on which they are modeled? These can be sold as collectibles too.

The nice thing about creating a collection of products and a line of accessories is that you literally have people lining up to buy those items before they're even being put up for sale. That's right. Think about the software games like Mario Brothers. Those cute little plumbers had all sorts of versions of that game being sold with different complexities to them. You mastered one and you had to get the next one!

That's how you establish a collection, by selling in series. You start with a few models and have some way to collect and display each item in the series. Then, every time you create a new item for your collection, you simply send out notification to all the people who have bought in the past from that collection. You don't have to go out and search out new customers. You don't have to constantly think up new products, just modify an existing one with different models. And, you can even charge more when you create some limited edition collectibles for discriminating collectors.

Timing this strategy

This strategy takes a little planning to have a line of products that can be consistently promoted as the next must have item in your customer's collections. Even though anything is collectible by somebody, obviously some market niches are more wide open than others. You may be able to find someone interested in collecting old drafting tools, but it's highly likely that this isn't a very big batch of people.

So, do a little research on each of your items before you decide to try to employ this strategy. It will take a little planning so that when you are promoting the products, you are promoting in the right series and as a collectible from the start. You will find that some categories of products lend themselves well to this strategy and can increase your sales easily. Things like prints, stamps, coins, vintage items, historical items, and art can be considered to have a wide appeal as collectibles. So, if you sell any of those, you want to focus on developing a collection of products and even create displays that you can send to your customers to promote the collecting bug to take root. As such, this strategy should be implemented by you when you decide to market a particular class of products and should be thought of as a long-range strategy.

It should be cross sold on the backend of a sale anytime anybody makes a purchase from the collection, by suggesting other items within the collection in between the time they have decided to buy one and confirmed the order. This can be just an extra page showing how the history of the collection is developed and other items people purchase with it, or it can be placed as an advertisement on the order form with a discount available for buying more than one in the collection.

Treat them oh so special

Everyone's heard of the posh restaurants that are so exclusive that you have to be somebody to get a reservation and even then, it may be for a seat months away. Yet, the very fact that a restaurant is so exclusive is the drawing card that keeps it booked and turning people away. They can then charge just about anything they want for their meals and many are infamous for providing plates that would make Minnie Mouse think she was on a diet. It doesn't matter though! What matters is how special you feel just showing up to the front desk and getting in. You know you're special and they treat you very, very special too.

When you walk in the restaurant has an ambiance of luxury and opulence. When you sit down, there is fine linen on the table and multiple sets of dinner ware. You are served complimentary bread, still warm from the oven, with perfectly cooled butter pats in ceramic crocks. The menus are custom made and elegant. The centerpiece is fresh flowers, artistically arranged for your pleasure. The people seated in the restaurant are all high class and well dressed. You know that you are seated there because you are part of that special class of people who managed to get a reservation. You're completely sold on the experience and odds are you'll pay several hundred dollars just to have dinner there.

That's the power of exclusivity.

Anything that is so hard to come by and creates an ambiance that is oh so special automatically appreciates in the buyer's estimation. We talked a little bit about this in the previous chapter, but that was for mass produced items that may be artificially manipulated into limited editions. Whereas a limited edition is a version of this strategy, this takes it one step further. You are going to make the scarcity or uniqueness of your item so obvious, and the experience of ownership so special, that people will fall all over themselves to be the ones to have that item in their possession.

The strategic plan

Okay, say you have a product that is so luxurious or outright ostentatious that you think you might have trouble convincing people that it's something they need or want. Maybe the cost to market it is beyond all the other prices of the products in your existing inventory. How can you justify the purchase when it is so obviously out of kilter with what most people expect or even need in their lives?

Well, you begin by informing your customers that you have this very special product. In fact, it's so special it's not just limited, it's downright scarce. Maybe, due to the fact that it is so special and hard to produce, only a certain number can be made or marketed at one time. After they're sold, you'll have to be put on a waiting list and it may be years before you get a chance to even buy one again.

Then you frame the benefits or features of this product by comparing it to the other products in your lineup to show just exactly how special this thing is. Maybe it has a bigger engine, way out of proportion to anything you really need, but that's the beauty of something that is "special." Maybe it is huge when compared to other products in the lineup. For instance, maybe you are selling a home with over 4,000 square feet, way more than you really need. That's what makes it special!

Remember that it can't just be a manufactured limited edition, even though that would be like a watered down version of this strategy. It's more a genuine reason why this product is so special that only a few people are going to get the opportunity and pleasure of experiencing it for themselves.

And, this doesn't have to just be about the product itself. Maybe there is another reason that the product has become clearly special over time. It has increased in value way out of proportion to other similar products because of some unique feature. For instance, maybe you are selling stamps with defects on them. They are special not because they outperform other stamps, but rather because they are highly unique in the stamp world and therefore worth more.

The psychological triggers

Going back to the restaurant example. This strategy holds a tremendous draw across all demographics because of the exclusivity factor. We all want to feel special and be recognized as special people. So, even though going to an exclusive restaurant could never be justified for the budget conscious, it will even attract people from this segment of the population. Why? Well, because the experience is so exclusive that it is seen as a "once in a lifetime" opportunity. And, who is dumb enough to skip that sort of offer? You either take it when it comes up, or you miss out on it possibly for good. It's no contest, most people will definitely try to scrounge up whatever resources they can just to be able to include that special event as a memory in their life.

What's more for items which have a physical nature to them, like exclusive editions of cars or art, you will see people use them as investments. They know that because something is rare, it will always be in demand. As the scarcity continues to drive up the price over time, the fact that they own one of the few remaining items means they might be able to sell it later for more money than they spent on it. Of course, that's not always the case, but many people can justify an exclusive edition of an item with this very logic.

How to implement effectively

Whereas some products are created to be exclusive, you can create an aura of exclusivity even for items that didn't start out that way. So, if you happen to sell used books, you may find that you have several that are out-of-print. Instead of making the book less valuable, the fact that it is now more exclusive gives you a way to market it so that it attracts more attention. You can talk about how it is now out-of-print and a very rare book. You can talk about how the paper it is printed on is indicative of its age or specialness, or even the typeset. Of course you have to educate your buyer so that they understand why you are selling the item as a special buy.

The more detail you give out about what makes this product unique, the more you will start to convince the reader that this is indeed a unique buying opportunity. If you happen to know how many other similar items exist in the world, then this is definitely information you need to relay to the reader to provide proof of exclusivity. For instance, say you are selling a stamp with a defect. You know that there were only so many of these stamps issued before the mistake was caught and corrected. Maybe you know how many people actually own a similar stamp. The thing is you want to include some actual numbers to make it obvious why this is a very exclusive stamp and exactly how much it has appreciated over time.

You can also include this strategy by targeting your collectors for the sale of the exclusive items as well as the limited editions. These are the people who are most motivated to make sure they have all of the models that come out of a specific product, so even though it may be a little more than they're willing to spend, it might just complete their collection or make it ultra-special. So, send out the notice of your exclusive item to your die-hard collectors first to see if you get any bites.

Finally, if you can point out an additional feature that brings your product exceptional value because it will never be created again, then you have a very exclusive item. Examples of this are books signed by dead authors. Obviously, you won't find new ones being created if the author is dead. That means that the signed copy is much more distinguished for its peer of unsigned copies because it also holds memorabilia in the form of a signature from a person of note.

Remember to price your item accordingly. If you say only six copies exist or will be made, you shouldn't come up with a seventh. It destroys your reputation completely as a reputable dealer. It may seem like a great idea to create more because people are paying such exorbitant prices for the few you did sell, but the only reason they did so was because they were convinced it was completely unique and exclusive. If later new ones come off the production line, they are bound to get very angry with you and even potentially sue you for false advertising.

To give the experience of having purchased something completely out-of-the-ordinary, you want to make sure it comes in special packaging. Like a diamond ring comes in a velvet box, you want to make sure your exclusive offers come packaged in high quality materials. Many times people who collect exclusive items won't even remove the packaging and it is more valuable this way. So, to give them the experience of having bought something special also remember to include special packaging.

One way to imprint the degree of specialness on the experience of owning something is to combine it with a certificate of authenticity. This is done with very exclusive prints that may only be sold in very small quantities. Even Franklin Mint will send certificates that come with the package to make sure that if the owner wants to resell the product that they can prove it is truly a Franklin Mint special edition.

Timing this strategy

The time to bring up the actual exclusivity of a product is actually before the sale, although that's not the only time when you will impact the buyer with the fact that they've made a special purchase. You want to be sure to frame the offer to show exactly how special your item is and give that as the reason why the buyer shouldn't delay on their decision to buy. If they hesitate, the opportunity will be lost and they'll never have another chance to buy the same item again!

The other time to make sure the buyer knows they've bought something special is after they've received the item. It should make them feel special when they get it. Otherwise, they will feel ripped off instead of recognized as the smart buyer they want to be. So, always seek to add special packaging, quality materials, and even certificates of authenticity whenever possible. They should have the experience that this is truly a product that stands out as one of a kind and extremely valuable and rare.

Tell them it's urgent

If you let your sales prospect leave to think over your sales promotion, odds are you've lost the sale. The main reason for this is that you didn't include a sense of urgency in your offer, and if you did, the sales prospect might have still hesitated at the end. If you've already raised the objections and resolved them and done some emotional salesmanship, then, why isn't your prospect ready to pull out their wallet now? You may not have relayed a sense of urgency crucial for them to make up their minds while you have them in your sight.

Think of it this way. If you are trying to get immediate action or attention from a crowd of people, you might try saying: "Excuse, excuse me..." into a nearby microphone. Odds, are they will ignore you and go about their business.

However, if you were to grab the microphone and yell, "Fire!" you can bet you've instigated immediate attention and action.

Similarly, you want your offers to light that fire under your sales prospects so they don't think they have time to ponder your offer. They must make up their minds right then and there. This dramatically increases the probability that you will close that sale.

The strategic plan

There's basically two themes to this strategy. You are either trying to light a fire at the beginning of the sales presentation or you are trying to overcome a final objection with a sense of urgency.

In the first case, where you are trying to light a fire at the beginning of the presentation, the idea is to make your sales offer dramatic and instantly appealing. That doesn't mean that you have to focus on positive aspects, as fear can also be a powerful motivator to buy. But, you do want to provoke a powerful emotional response that invokes the potential for a huge loss if the person doesn't take immediate action.

No one likes to feel like they are losing something because they weren't bold enough to take action now. You also want them to become engaged in the buying experience so that they want to become the hero of their own drama and resolve that problem that's plagued them and driven them to your sales page. However, if you don't bolster their courage or show them that it is possible, then they might feel strange jumping up to grab your offer, even if emotionally they are ready to do so. So, give them a little push.

One of the best ways to create a sense of urgency to give a time limit to the offer or make it a special "introductory" offer. The time limited offers will work for new and existing customers, whereas the introductory offer is great for people who are new to your site and may need a push to commit to the first sale. Either way, the way this strategy would work is that you are creating an expectation of loss if the person doesn't take you up on their offer at that moment. In the case of an introductory offer, it may be one-time available to people who subscribe to your mailing list. If they don't take you up on it then, later the same offer will be priced much higher.

In the case of the limited offers, the loss expressed may be that you won't be able to even offer the same package at a later date. Once it's sold out, it's gone. Or, once the time limit is reached, you'll no longer offer that package again at that price. Here the loss is expressed as either a price or an opportunity to own a particular product package. So, the sense of urgency is increased dramatically when there is a potential for loss either in monetary or opportunity.

In the second case, you have just sold Mrs. Smith on a great new dishwasher, when she says she wants to go home and think about it or discuss it with her husband. If you let Mrs. Smith walk out and do not resolve that objection with a sense of urgency, you've lost the sale. The second case is much trickier to implement, and we will go over it more in depth in the implementation segment, however, you will want to make sure that you direct a sense of urgency and a personal sense of loss to the potential buyer considering buying your product. Otherwise, once you make it personal, they won't need anyone else's opinion to decide whether the purchase is a good idea or not. Empower them to make their own buying decisions!

The psychological triggers

The species as a whole is programmed to avoid loss and danger, otherwise, we'd have had a tough time staying alive. So, subconsciously we are constantly monitoring our environment for cues that might suggest that we could be in danger or that we will be experiencing a dramatic loss and to flee or evade the problem as quickly as possible.

And, in fact, our nervous system is fine-tuned to make us react much more quickly at signs of danger or loss. You hear the stories of the mothers who have lifted whole cars off their babies who got caught underneath in superhuman efforts of strength and courage. Why? The idea of the loss of their child was so unbearable that nervous system kicked in to give them the boost they needed to overcome that problem. It made them act in bolder ways to take action immediately.

While losing money or an opportunity can't be compared with the potential of losing a child, the same dynamics are at play. It creates a sense of urgency if there is a possible loss of money or opportunity. The greater the potential loss, the more the nervous system kicks in to take immediate action. That's why most financial experts warn that people are risk adverse and shouldn't watch the stock market. If they do and see their investments drop substantially, they pull their money out instead of waiting for the market to correct. That's because the loss triggered a subconscious risk that caused them to take immediate and usually a highly emotional action, rather than to think the other options out.

This works for sales because if you give your prospect time to think about the other options, odds are they'll either think up more objections to your products or decide to buy someone else's product. It may not even be a better product, just better marketed. If they aren't given a reason in every single presentation why they shouldn't walk away and think about, this can be the most damaging of objections to your sales effort because once you are out of sight, it's guaranteed you are out of mind! All that effort for nothing!

How to implement effectively

Your sales copy will have to invoke a sense of urgency since you do not have the prospect in front of you as in a retail store situation. You can do this as boldly or as subtly as you like. You can simply call some offers "introductory" and not say anything about whether the price will change or not, however, just that word implies something will change down the line. Or you can very clearly state that it is a one-time or time limited offer as a more direct way of creating urgency.

However, there are even more creative ways you can invoke a sense of loss that have nothing to do with time. That's what makes them so effective. You aren't necessarily rushing anyone, but the implication is that if they don't rush themselves, they will experience a loss that may be unrecoverable. An example of this would be if you have a product that is giving companies who buy it a competitive edge. So, you can explain how everyone uses it and why it increases productivity and provides that competitive edge. Then, you can suggest all of the major players who have bought your product and how the sales prospect shouldn't delay, so as to remain competitive in their business. Well, there is no actual time frame that you've mentioned or a time limit on your offer, but you've very effectively lit a fire under most business owner's butts due to the potential for loss of business to other well-equipped establishments.

Another way to invoke a sense of urgency is when it's a matter of style or status. When is the best time to get something novel that really sets you above your peers? When the product first comes out. If it is predicted to be a hot seller, then you have to get one before it sells out! This marketing strategy can even help with pre-sales, so that you can reserve orders before the product is even out. If people think the demand will be huge, you can even sell the reservation by asking them to put money down to hold their order and guarantee delivery by a certain date.

This type of logic is also used when marketers say: "Be the first to own this fully loaded cell phone." Or, whatever the product might be. They are hoping to increase your sense of urgency by getting people to jostle for being the first in line to buy their product. After all, once everyone has one then it's not such a big deal anymore and the urgency is lost.

Framing your offer in a way that creates some impulse to take the action to buy when the copy is read is very important to online sales. If you don't get that urgency across, people will drift off to some other site or activity and may even forget where they last saw that offer.

In retail sales, one of the worst objections one can hear is the person who insists that before they can buy something they have to check with their spouse. Why? Well, it puts the marketer in the difficult position of being completely unable to create that sense of urgency to make the purchase while they are still standing there. In those situations, if the marketer doesn't act fast, they will lose the sale for sure. So, that's when they have to get a bit personal. They have to be a little bold too. They might even dare to ask the person if their husband or wife makes all their buying decisions for them? They may want to know if the husband or wife checks with them in all their major purchases too? Or, they might want to know if it's really necessary to get approval for a purchase that may have nothing to do with a spouse.

Now, you would think that getting nosy and personal is going to have a poor reaction. It might, but you know already that if you let that person leave your store with that objection, you've lost the sale for sure. So, what do you have to lose?

Online, the same strategy isn't as important since you aren't face-to- face with a person, but even so, you want to make sure that the visitor understands why it is personally important for them to make that purchase now, without checking in with others. This is easy to do if the products are gender-based like woman's toiletries or men's ties. You make sure your customer is aware that women with taste or men with sense know that it is a great deal that they shouldn't pass up!

Timing this strategy

This is one strategy that should ALWAYS be attempted in conjunction with other strategies. It certainly can't hurt to try and light a fire under your sales prospect's rear end to get them to buy.

Gain trust with your credentials

Now, if you make an offer (no matter how incredibly good it may be), you won't attract sales if no one believes you can deliver what you offered. That's because people need to trust you before they will make a purchase from you. And, if the purchase is something that appears too good to be true, and they don't know you, they simply won't believe you are telling the truth.

Like any relationship, you have to build trust over time by delivering what you promise. So, what can you do for those that have yet to buy and haven't even entered into a commercial relationship with you? Well, you can flash your credentials!

Have you ever noticed that when people find out you are a doctor, they automatically assume you are smarter and richer than the average person? That's because your profession gives you credentials to be a person of integrity and a productive member of society.

Education is one way that people flash credentials, by putting the initials to their degrees next to their names. There are certain ways to establish your credentials with your website audience that can be used to get them to trust you more and, thus, help you make the sale.

The strategic plan

The nature of this strategy is to create a tone of authenticity and authority. You want to sound believable, educated, maybe even an expert about a particular topic related to your market niche. When people find someone who they can trust to tell them the truth exactly like it is, then they are more easily influenced into following the advice that person gives.

You will want to invoke associations that enhance your image as a knowledgeable and credible person and reduce the associations to those things that may impinge on your good name. Both of these aspects are looked at quite closely when a customer is trying to make a decision whether you are steering them in the right direction or just trying to make a fast buck.

You will have to pay attention to the language that you use in your sales copy. It shouldn't contain any outrageous claims or even untruthful exaggerations. You want to highlight the benefits of your product or service, but in a manner that comes off as genuine, not hyped.

There are a number of different ways to implement this strategy, to help you build your credibility quickly and effectively, however, the strategy is still the same. You want to remove the objections in your customers mind to the possibility that they are being taken for a ride or influenced in underhanded ways. You do this by seeking to make sure your transactions always have a high degree of integrity from sale to delivery, and that you back everything with your good name.

The psychological triggers

This strategy works because we are conditioned to trust those people who have certain authority over us. As children, our parents are invested with that authority and we're taught to believe everything they say, and more importantly, that they have our good interest at heart. That is where we first learn to trust in an authority figure.

Later, we learn that this same dynamic extends to our bosses, our spouses, and even to people with education or some measure of success in their lives. We assume that if someone has made it to a certain level in society than their word tends to carry weight because they are more experienced and know how to ride the rapids of life. So, we may be automatically triggered to respect an authority figure, but that doesn't necessarily mean we automatically trust them.

Unless you are co-dependent, most people will make other people earn their trust in order engage a healthy relationship.

No one wants to be used or abused by people in authority, just because they claim to know better for us. In those instances, we may be triggered, but we can also completely rebel against the idea and dig in our heels and refuse to comply with the direction given. And, that's a perfectly healthy reaction to protect the person from being taken advantage of.

Similarly, online sales people may expound on their credentials all day long and even impress their visitors, but they still have to put their money where their mouth is and act with integrity to gain their trust. If someone hasn't directly interacted with you, than they may decide to ask someone else whether you deliver what you promise. That's called a referral and is another way credibility is built. So, even though you have no direct history with someone it doesn't mean you can't create the atmosphere necessary to get people to trust you enough to buy from you.

You can do that by paying close attention to the image you project online. You have to make sure that it is as authentic to the products and services that you promote. That means that if you sell sports gear and you've never even picked up a tennis racket in your life or played a team sport, you will be completely lacking in credibility unless you get other noted sports figures to become your spokesperson. Then, your business has more credibility even though you personally may have none in that particular niche market.

So, authenticity is the name of the game in Web 2.0 online businesses. You will see this becoming more and more important as social networking takes over the Internet. When people social network, they talk to each other based on friendships they've developed with people they trust.

So, when they go out to buy something they often know at least someone online who can give them a good idea of whether your claims are credible and your business trustworthy. If you scam people, odds are in this Internet age, your online business will not last long. People tend to notify and warn people in their circle of friends quite quickly in social networking sites and can directly impact your bottom line.

How to implement effectively

So, the first thing you want to do is make sure that the copy on your site is truthful. No claims that cannot be supported. If you say free delivery, then keep to your word and don't sneak in a shipping and handling fee. Next, you will want to keep away from marketing clichés that give people the impression of the snake oil vendors of the past. Its one thing to make a claim that may seem unbelievable, but can be backed by hard facts, and quite another just to splatter outrageous claims all over your website without trying to justify them.

That brings us to the next thing you need to do to implement this strategy. That is, you need to handle the customer's objections, which might be in their mind, as efficiently and accurately as possible. If one of the objections is that the price is too high, then don't try to hide that fact, but justify why it is high in a credible way. If the sales prospect may still have problems believing the claims, which are indeed true, then you need to trot out the authority figures, whether you or someone else.

Take for instance a product that is a medical device of some sort and it claims to get rid of acne or some such thing, then you will want to be able to back that claim with either a doctor's credentials or clinical trials. Use the types of credentials that our society agrees gives one authority: degrees, awards, and even personal success. If it is an info- product that shows how you made money on the Internet, you had better be able to pull out whatever evidence to show that you were indeed highly successful using those methods, whether it is bank statements or you annual statement for PayPal.

You can build up an image of an expert on the Internet very quickly. That's because content is so important to drive search engine results. If you know that your market niche is being heavily searched by surfers, you can start to write multiple articles and submit them to article directories to create a bigger name for yourself online. Many of these article directories allow you a resource box that you can put your website address in to bring in traffic from these sites. This serves a two-fold purpose: you become an instant expert on the Internet, and you drive more traffic to your site. It's a great way to build credibility.

If you still have trouble building some credibility, then think about writing free guest posts for sites that already have a big audience and a high degree of credibility. By doing so, you gain traffic and polish up your online image by associating with noted experts or successful online marketers or bloggers. In this way, they lend you some of their credibility for contributing to their site. You can also do mini versions of this by simply commenting on open blogs with informational comments that make you look good. Don't forget to add a link to your site to generate more traffic too!

If you don't have time for all that, you can simply pay someone to endorse your products, as mentioned earlier. You can do this by using celebrity endorsements or simply getting someone in the business with great credibility to write a review of your site or products. Once they give their endorsement, their credibility rubs off on you, virtually overnight! A limited version of this is to pay people to let you advertise on their sites with a link back to your site. They aren't necessarily endorsing you, but the association with their site will reap a similar effect, just watered down somewhat.

Certain geographical regions might lend more credibility to a product than others. For instance, remember when made in Japan made it was junk? Well, when cars started rolling off the Asian assembly lines the fact that they were imported from Japan finally gave them more credibility, not less, but it took time for that impression of trustworthiness to seep into the cultural consciousness. Also, you know that certain places are known for having excellent products – like wine from France and cheese from Wisconsin. If you are selling items that can gain credibility from their place of origin, be sure to mention it! Even your company can gain credibility at times from its place of business, just like the best publishing houses are all known to reside in New York City.

One thing to remember is that if you are the expert on your products, than you know what makes them so special and such a good deal. All you have to do is be able to convey that to your customers in a genuine and friendly fashion for them to start believing it too. And, when the sale is made, don't stop there! Be sure that you pay the same attention to the integrity of the entire sales process so that your customers will know that your word means something and they can expect to get exactly what you promised or you will make good on it. That type of customer service will have them coming back over and over and referring all their friends to you too!

Timing this strategy

You will need to work a little to get this strategy going. It should be planned for even before you have a website up and running and selling products. You should start building your professional image immediately online through social networking sites, building an expert blog, and writing articles if you expect to use your own image to sell your products.

Obviously, your credentials can be added to with every achievement in your life. Be sure to add multiple online profiles that talk about your achievements all with links back to the website when it goes up. Always continue to update your credentials every time you receive some new recognition, award, degree, or have a very successful campaign! The name of the game is to toot your own horn!

You should also have an "About Me" section in all of your websites to make sure people know you are trustworthy. Include that information in the copy too, if you are using this strategy to invoke authority and credibility to sell your products. It should be easy to find this information almost immediately if that's the impact you want to make.

This is a never-ending process once you start as your image is what is being used to sell your products, you will want to protect it. You need to constantly monitor your affiliates, your customer service representatives, and your own claims to make sure they are truthful and trustworthy people. Associate with the wrong crowd for too long, and the reputation can shift just like the tail winds of a hurricane. So, keep at it and you can reap a sterling reputation that helps sell your products simply through the virtue of honesty and integrity.

Make it cozy and familiar

As we have already discussed, you can often sell things through the associations you make with it. Now we are going to discuss how linking your product to things that are familiar to your customers can help to breed a cozy familiarity that is appealing. For products that are new, it can even be a way to overcome the resistance to buying if you link the product with something they already know.

One of the easiest ways to do this type of association is to link your products to some cultural phenomena or fad that is currently in the forefront of the mass consciousness. Once it is associated with some fad, by default your product also gains tremendous popularity along with the fad. However, you do have to be careful that when a trend ends, that your sales don't dwindle too. The positive aspects of linking to a popular subject are obvious, but the negative aspects can sometimes be ignored and impact your sales. So, remain aware that you always have to understand that linking your product to other cultural trends works both ways.

The strategic plan

You will want to identify what trends are foremost in the mind of your visitors. They could be cultural, ethnic, behavioral, or simply a shift in the public's awareness. As an example, if you are selling kid's toys and there is a popular television series that has enormous popularity, if you can link your product to this series, you will experience good growth in your sales.

Your product doesn't even have to be directly related to the event that you are exploiting, for it to work. As long as it draws attention – even controversy – to your sales ad. Online controversy is a sure way to gain attention even if it can be explosive. If you understand how to manipulate a controversy to your advantage, you can even use these controversies to sell your products. At the very least, you will increase your site's traffic.

Sometimes an event is a good thing to link your products to, like a historical event. This is actually done around major holidays when all sort of Christmas-themed wares and/or gifts show up in the stores. But, beyond the holidays there are events that can influence your visitors to buy your products: Earth Day for greenies, for instance.

Highly controversial or anticipated events can be great product promoters. The American national elections, for instance, is a giant boom for people who sell items with logos. Now, they can sell T- shirts, bumper stickers, and all sorts of different types of products by linking them to either the Republican or the Democratic candidates. As different controversies erupt over the candidates it can be a gold mine for people who want to show their party loyalties through the products they buy.

But, this strategy isn't just relegated to fads and controversies, it's also about making new products or unusual products more familiar and cozy. An example of this is an ad that was printed in the past selling smoke detectors that look intimidatingly high-tech which compared it to a very sensitive nose. Suddenly, the smoke detector wasn't so odd and frightening, but rather familiar to the average human being. In the process, the smoke alarm is reframed to something that a person can rely on every day to keep them out of danger without being too concerned about the mechanics of it.

The psychological triggers

By associating products with things that already are prominently within the conscious mind of your buyers, it captures more attention from your market. Our minds are constantly filtering out vast amounts of input from many different sources: the media, our friends and relatives, and even the Internet. We have learned to multitask quite well, but at the same time we don't quite pay full attention to everything that comes across our visual screen. So, in order to really grab our attention something has to trigger either a deep familiarity to bypass the filters that throw out garbage inputs, or it has to stir such a controversy that it produces an emotional impact that also busts through your thinking filters.

Human beings are also creatures of habit. They go to sleep on the same side of the bed every night and wake up and brush their teeth in the morning without fail. This type of routine is comforting to people and helps people to manage their lives, their emotions, and their thoughts. Once you've got an established lifestyle that makes you comfortable, you are pretty set in your ways and typically don't want to mess up a good thing. So, why would you switch from your morning cup of coffee to some other beverage? Why would you opt to eat a new toaster croissant, when your old bagels are just as yummy and you've been eating them for years? The fact is that people won't just jump to try new things without first deciding whether they even understand why they'd want to in the first place. The familiarity of the old things are comforting and it takes a lot of momentum to change to something new.

That's why linking new products to old things that are familiar works to sell them better. You're not really selling a new, strange, animal that no one has ever used before, you're selling an improved version of the same, old, classic, and dependable item they've come to know and love. You aren't just asking them to believe you that this new thing will make their lives better, they already know it has and now they can even improve that experience up a notch too. This makes new things that may be difficult to sell because of their strange new offering a much more appealing prospect.

Linking also works on the memory as this is exactly how people recall things in their long-term memory, by linking them to other memories that are more easily recalled. So, even if you don't sell the prospect immediately, your sales ad makes an emotional impact on the psyche that is stored much longer in the memory of the reader and more easily recalled later.

Finally, associating your products with dramatic events or culturally recognized phenomena also lends your products an air of controversy. For those that harbor the inner rebel, they will jump on your band wagon just to be included as part of that anti-culture movement. So, even for those that think they are evading the propensity of human beings to stick with what they know, this strategy can work by linking the product to the thing they know and dislike and then providing it as part of the anti-culture solution.

How to implement effectively

There are various ways to implement this strategy. For a new product that has unbelievable claims because it is so novel, you'll want to link it to something familiar and comforting. These types of items shouldn't be linked with controversy because they're controversial enough.

For existing products that you just want to build a campaign employing this strategy, you can brainstorm all of the current events, cultural phenomena, news items and fads that might be able to be used to sell this product. If you are trying to sell a product with a new feature you can link it to the old product or something familiar to help them accept the new feature.

A more subtle way to associate something that's familiar with a positive framework is to use common items that are held in high esteem to get the message across that this is something worthwhile to possess. For example, the words diamond, gold, and platinum are used in a variety of products and even memberships to link those qualities associated with these items to other products and services. Ever hear of platinum spark plugs? They go for about $60 each. That's what the power of a little clever linking can do for you. It can not only make something seem more familiar, but it also gets some of the same aura of qualities of the items you've associated with it. So, in a sense, you've manipulated the potential buyer's perception of quality by associating it with familiar, but luxurious, elements in nature.

If you can use some of the terms that are being used in the fad to help link your item to the more popular item, it will be easily associated and understood to be linking to it. Like when Star Wars was big, anything that used some of the classic sayings of this blockbuster film was instantly recognized. Yoda sayings in particular were an excellent way to tie into popular culture and still be able to use them in your marketing efforts. Spoofs and take-offs from the saying "The force is with you" were humorous and eye-catching.

The way this strategy can really take off is if you link to something that is in the current news media. If there is a controversy over some news piece, like when women burned their bras, then link your product or service to that particular controversy to get some instant media attention. You don't even have to be for or against the controversy or in women's lingerie. When women burned their bras there were even pizza places baking pizzas shaped like bras, in order to garner attention – and, it worked!

So, while you want to associate with different cultural phenomena, even controversy, it doesn't have to be all that serious. You don't have to take sides, and often it's better if you don't. If you take one side, you lose the other side as potential customers. So, the best way to implement this is to make a social statement without offending people while you are at it.

Timing this strategy

This strategy is reserved for when you are making the pitch for your product or service. You can't really link two things together, if one of the items (your product) remains an unknown. So, there is a bit of a tightrope you are walking here. You want to associate with some powerful symbol in the mass media, but you don't necessarily want it to overwhelm your sales pitch. Remember that the reason you are using the strategy is to sell your product or service, not to promote some cause or movie.

So, this strategy works well as press releases and other mass media items that draw attention, but also talk about your own product too. You can continue to use the same strategy on your sales page, but also list all the benefits of your product and use the strategy to introduce your product first. That way, people who found out about your product from searching for terms related to the mass symbol, will be able to quickly shift from that thing to your own products and services with a great degree of familiarity and comfort. If done correctly, this strategy is a smooth way to lead huge amounts of traffic from other sites to your sales pages.

Connect them with their people

Innate in the human culture is the desire to belong. Whether we want to belong to our families, our heritage, our country, or some other group, the desire is very strong and appealing. And, in sales, when you create an image of a particular brand the people who end up buying that comprise a status group of peers with like-minded values. This can be very attractive to people who seek always to establish a connection that affirms their own identities.

In social networking, the number one reason people are engaged on these sites is their desire to express their identity. Part of that is joining groups of like-minded souls, frequenting places that these people go, and even buying the same things these people buy. So, even though the action may be instigated by their own identity, the final strong desire is a need to belong.

The strategic plan

If you understand this basic need to belong, and you know what products your visitors are buying, you can easily provide the solution for that need by highlighting all qualities that take into account that particular group's identity. In addition, once you understand which demographic your potential buyer belongs to, you also know by association which other products and services would appeal to them. So, you can increase your sales just with this one insight and by facilitating the ability for people to identify with their preferred groups. And, once you have a large grouping of people or products with brands that reflect a certain set of people's values or aspirations, then this will draw even more people to the offer who are completely invested in belonging to that particular group.

So, you do need to do research on the demographics of your visitors. If you are already in business, you will have a good idea what sorts of values and services they are buying into. This will give you an idea of the type of grouping that might be the people they wish to identify with. Of course, just because one belongs to a particular group because of personal demographics, it doesn't necessarily mean that is the group they want to be associated with when buying. It just gives you a starting point.

For instance, in the 2008 United States elections, the Democratic Party was always associated with equal opportunity. They had several candidates running for the party's nomination, from a black man to a woman. The Republicans were seen as less for equal opportunity until they put a woman on the ticket for their vice- presidential candidate. If this were a sale and the product is the presidency, what they are doing is trying to get the swing voters, independents and democrats, to identify more with their party through adding a female as a statement on equal opportunity. They know that the demographic of swing voters are mostly white, older, women who are not happy with Hillary Clinton not being on the Democratic ticket. So, even though that's the demographic, they included a young, white, woman to the description of the ticket to stir up excitement for the Republican ticket, not just from older white women, but from younger voters too.

Similarly, luxury products may be primarily aimed at wealthy buyers, but there is a whole class of people who would like to be associated with the affluent, whether they have the budget for it or not. So, the starting point is the demographic of people who are considered affluent, since they need to be connected to their status group. However, in advertising and marketing, you also have to make it easier for those that want to identify with the group, but lack a key demographic trait to make the switch too.

You can do this either by branding a line of products, with the potential to increase your association as your circumstances change, or by clearly defining the values and qualities of that product with the people who buy it. Then, you continue to cultivate that connection by offering other products and services that those people associate with the grouping of people that they desire to be a part of.

The psychological triggers

There's a number of reasons this strategy is so effective. The most obvious is the natural desire to be accepted as part of a group to increase your chances of prospering, both socially and financially. When times are really tough, that's when people gather together into like-minded groups for the sake of survival. That's what the basic family unit is all about, and that dynamic lasts until the day we take our last breath. A person without friends is a person who more than likely feels worthless. And, a person with many friends who affirm their identity, is a very blessed person indeed.

There are even scientific studies that show that our ability to heal and the joy we have in our lives is directly related to how many social interactions we maintain. People with a wide circle of friends, connections from church, family, and even professional organizations, can withstand the low periods in life much better than those without this type of emotional support in their lives. So, when someone feels they are identified with a particular group and are accepted with in it, it builds their confidence, their self-esteem, and increases their joy in life. Some medical studies even suggest it boosts their immune systems.

All of these things are felt emotionally as a very huge degree of satisfaction, and it's that feeling that is what pulls in prospects when you use this strategy. It makes them feel affirmed, connected, confident, and worthy to be included in the group of buyers who can achieve to own that particular thing you've associated with a status group.

Then, there is the interesting dynamic of camouflage that exists in nature and the human species. When, you don't have what it takes to actually belong to a particular group (like a chameleon that wants to be a part of a particular environment, but is really just a lizard), then the next best thing is to fake it to fool people into believing you actually are a twig, a leaf, or a high-status achiever. Even if you don't really belong to that group, the fact that you are identified with it confers on you the same privileges and status, and sometimes connections, which the others who do truly belong there get. That can heftily increase the probability of enhancing and later confirming an image of success.

How to implement effectively

The key to implementing this strategy in a way that wows your customers is to treat them as if they already belong to the group they desire to be a part of. If they aren't particularly wealthy, but they are looking to buy a luxury car from you, then being treated as such will help to build the desire to make the purchase from you and really belong to the group.

Another way to do this is that when someone buys a brand that is associated with a particular group, like greenies who like conservation and saving the rain forest, then you have a very good idea of what else they would like. You should suggest those items to them, and in fact, you can do it even before the sale is finalized. You suggest products that complement the sale or you can even show how some of the other products you sell also go towards saving the rain forest. You can even ask them to upgrade to be more ecologically conscious.

Let's face it, we tend to like to join cliques of people who can agree with most of our values, even if we don't really have the credentials to belong. Like a person who goes in to buy a luxury car without enough money to finance the purchase, they don't want to be called out for being somewhere they don't belong. Instead, they want to be accepted for the part so much, that they will sometimes even make the sale to prove they belong and can work the part.

You can implement this strategy when you decide to create lists of people to market specific products or brands online. You can have different mailings go to different groupings, each one stating how the new products or services you are offering help them to identify more with their status group. A very powerful technique to then implement is peer pressure. Suggest that other people who bought a particular item also found that they desired other items. You can even purchase marketing lists from people, if you want to include direct mail in your campaigns, that help you to target specific groups, and cross- reference them with other lists or groupings too.

One can't really leave this conversation, without mentioning how social networking has become the cornerstone of this strategy online. Social networking sites like Facebook are set up to neatly get people joining into circle of friends with similar interests. As you start establishing profiles on these sites, you begin to notice that some friends all use the same applications or enjoy putting similar items on their profiles. This gives you great insight into the types of items that they might purchase, if given the chance. While you can't solicit people on social networking sites effectively, you can create links on your profile to offers that are targeted to help these people find a product or service that is branded for their interests.

You can also set up different groups and there you can solicit and market people more than on individual profiles. Social Ads in Facebook are a very finely tuned way to market specific demographics of people and connect them with the offers that help them to identify with their people.

If you can offer your customers something that allows them to flaunt their peer status, this can also help you finalize the offer. This is how education, such as degrees and certificates, are sold. People want to connect with other people who have similar interests and learn and grow more through them. But, when it comes time to use it, they want that sheepskin so they can tell everyone that they are an accomplished member of a specific and special group, and they now have the credentials to prove it.

So, if you are selling items like workshops or online courses, it helps to give out certificates of accomplishment that people can display to others. Online, you can even make up virtual badges and awards that people can post on their electronic profiles or web pages, that show they have become a member of a prestigious group, even if the only qualification is to simply buy a product from you. Then, you can amp that marketing strategy even more by providing a link back to your products, services, or website from the virtual award or badge. This generates more traffic for you and more chances to sell based on this strategy, since it will attract just the sort of people that this appeals to.

Timing this strategy

Since this strategy works through the power of image, you can use it practically anywhere in the sales cycle. You can sell pre-sales by the use of badges or sending specific notices to potential demographics and telling them the reason they were singled out is because they belong on your list. Maybe you were looking for engineers, nurses, or greenies, it doesn't matter. They'll be flattered to be recognized for being a part of that particular social identity and will give your offer serious thought.

You can use it on the sales page in your list of benefits. You can use it as an introductory offer to specific people who meet certain criteria. You can offer it as part of the incentive to join your special forums and groups, to meet up with like-minded folks. Then, you can market those groups quite easily for specific products and services that enhance that image.

You can set up profiles on social networking sites and create articles that highlight your own association with a particular group, making you an expert within the group. Once you create a circle of friends who are totally in line with that social peer group, you can start to bridge them to your website or to an intermediary blog where you can actually market them.

Finally, don't forget that you can add suggestions in emails, on the order form, and even the thank you page after an order is filled out. This strategy is so powerful that the more you use it, the more the buyers actually like it. They never get tired of it because it affirms their personal identities. So, unlike other strategies that needs specific timing and locations, this one is one that can be used anywhere and anytime with astounding results.

CHAPTER 5

ULTIMATE TRAFFIC PART III - PROSPECT TO CUSTOMER

Add a touch of guilt

Most friendships or transactions work on an ideal of reciprocity. When someone does something for you, you know there is an underlying expectation that the favor will someday be returned. In capitalism, when we go out and buy something, we typically exchange cash for a purchase. So the ideal of reciprocity exists in the commerce system too. Since that is the way we live, it often brings out a feeling of guilt if we take something and don't give something in return. That's the basis of this next strategy that can be used to trigger behavior to help you market and sell your products online.

The strategic plan

In order to trigger a sense of guilt that leads to a purchase, you have to frame your sales offer in a way that brings out the ideal of reciprocity in the sales prospect, in a very subtle way. If you actually try to guilt trip them in obvious manners, this strategy can backfire as no one likes to be manipulated. So, while you are going to actually do things that seem like a "nice extra" to your customer, it's actually going to send out the message: "I've scratched your back, now you scratch mine."

Now, some people are much more guilt-prone than others, even if everyone holds a basic ideal of a fair exchange. On the Internet, in particular, there are hordes of people who want offers for free and have no shame taking them without giving anything of value in return. These people are even as shameless as providing sham email addresses in exchange for free newsletter or reports that they can't get otherwise. Once they receive the free products, they simply destroy the "throwaway" email. And, there's little guilt involved. So, you want to be able to target people who not only feel a little guilt at receiving free offers, but it will also trigger buying behavior too. The most effective way to use guilt is to create an invisible lasso of obligation that literally pulls the prospective buyer to close on your offer.

Then, there are many others who appear immune to your tries to guilt-trip them into buying. That's because of the way people have become quite jaded about returning anything of value for a free offer, and so you have to work harder by repeating free offers, and also you have to vary the offers too. A free newsletter in exchange for an email may have worked in the past, but now it's not as easy to start putting people in a sales funnel as easily. So, you need to be creative in the freebies you give and how they are procured.

You do want whatever you decide to giveaway, whether it is a stamp, a coupon, or an expensive briefcase to have something to do with the product you are trying to sell, even though any small gift in the right setting can help you to sell anything through bribing people into a state of compliance and provide you an interested ear for your sales offers.

The psychological triggers

The pull of a bribe is so powerful that there are even laws against it in social and corporate politics. A bribe is usually something someone gives you with an underlying expectation that in the future you will do something that they want you to do. It is usually done with a basic understanding that you are willing to give favoritism in exchange for a gift. Well, that's really not far from what you're attempting to do here, except it's perfectly legal in some cases. You don't want to violate any ethical or legal provisions, if you are dealing with clients who can't receive gifts, but other than that, it's up to you to decide what you want to give away.

Generally, the bigger a gift is, the more sense of obligation people perceive they have towards you. So, if you are trying to sell something large, like a timeshare, the gift tends to be free weekends at a resort. These are large gifts that prime you into feeling cheap if at the end of your stay, you refuse to sign on the dotted line to buy the timeshare at the resort. However, you'll notice they call it a "free stay" and that the only obligation is that you attend a sales seminar at the end. That really puts the hint in prospective buyer's head that it really isn't free, even if it is labeled free.

People also like to reciprocate in kind. That means, if someone lends you money, they usually want to pay you back with money. On the other hand, if they help you to move your household goods when you buy a house, the underlying expectation is that when they move, you will be there for them too. Money is not the underlying expectation. So, you want to set up the offer so that they understand how they are reciprocating in kind, and then ask them for that sale.

Just in case they don't get it the first time, you can give them multiple gifts and built up the sense of guilt over time. They will either think you are one of the nicest sites online or that they really should start thinking about buying from you to pay you back before the subconscious guilt becomes overwhelming.

How to implement effectively

In order to see how to implement this strategy, there are many examples in sales you can review. The idea of salespeople taking their clients to lunch or dinner is a form of this strategy that makes the clients more susceptible to closing a sale. Another example is when you get a free newspaper, without obligation to buy. You'll see these stands at different venues like grocery stores. There, a person asks if you'd like a free newspaper. Then, when you go to pick it up, they ask you if you have a subscription and engage you in a sales transaction. It should be pretty obvious that you don't have a subscription, otherwise, you wouldn't bother to pick up a newspaper, but the idea isn't to determine whether you have it, but to engage you in a conversation that leads to them presenting their subscription offers. All for the price of a free newspaper that they hope will guilt you into buying the subscription.

Similarly, you want your freebie to be a segue way into your offers. You also want something that can stimulate the desire to buy as well as guilting people into it. Then, it can be a very powerful strategy.

For instance, sometimes you will get free stands or display cases for people who sell collector's items. The bigger and more elegant the display case, the more likely that you will not only feel pleasure, but also a certain amount of guilt for having received such a nice gift. The combination of these two emotions will lead you to buy more from the company, not only to pay them back but to also show off your collection in that really nice display case.

Charities know how to use this strategy quite well. They will send out mailings asking for donations and include small gifts like stamps, stickers, or even address labels within the mailing. Not only are people more likely to open the mailing to get to the goodies, but they are also more likely to donate too.

Online, you can use the same strategy by offering to give people free information in the form of reports or newsletters. You can even use email to send out weekly messages that can either be entertaining or informational. Just be sure that people have given you permission to be contacted by email so that it doesn't get you into trouble. This develops a relationship with your subscription holders. If your information proves to be valuable or entertaining people will want to read it and then you can market them for other offers.

In order to keep the freebie on target, they generally contain information that is in accordance with your market niche. That way, it not only gives the buyer a sense of guilt but also primes the way for other products like eBooks. You can even advertise other offers within the reports to help set the stage to sell them.

Software sellers know how to use this strategy pretty well by allowing people to download either demo versions or free trials so that the potential customer gets to experience the product for a short time or on a limited features basis. Often, once the trial ends, the person is so hooked on the product they will register to buy it and be grateful for the chance to try it out beforehand.

Another great way to stimulate a sense of guilt is to go the extra mile for your customers. If people feel you are making an extra effort just for them, then they not only feel special, but also more interested in reciprocating in the relationship. You can give them MORE than what they expect to receive and tell them it is a free gift just because. This almost always works to cement a good relationship.

Even the appearance of giving more than what you promised will also stimulate a sense of obligation. For instance, you have a great package that includes various reports, templates, videos, and an eBook. The entire package could be worth $99.95, but instead of selling it for that, you sell it for $59.95 and you let everyone know that you're only charging for the eBook, and everything else is a free gift; A bribe? Of course!

Now, you've not only given something away for free in their eyes, but you also made a BIG EFFORT in providing everything they need to have to solve their problems. You've done all the work of putting all the pieces together for them, and this can also produce a profound sense of obligation as well as connection.

The extra effort can also be something as small as adding something nice to the sale when it is delivered, and letting the customer know it was added intentionally. Some marketers add candy, but this can melt and get sticky in the summer when it is mailed. And, it's not associated with the products you sell, unless you happen to sell candy online. So, try to stick to things that people appreciate and that will help them to think of your products. If you are selling office supplies, you can always add additional freebies to the order like a large paper clip with your URL imprinted on it. It's not only a way of inducing a little touch of guilt, but it also is a way to remind them where to order their office supplies next time they run out.

Timing this strategy

The timing for this strategy is typically before any sales pitch has been made. Although, as we just discussed, it can be used after a sale is completed as well. If you use it before the sales pitch has been made, you may have to do it several times to get the trigger to go off.

The Internet makes it very easy to allow people to sign up to get free articles, videos, or other electronic formats in exchange for an email address. At that point, you are not asking for anything in return, even if the email address is what you are truly after. You are simply giving away things that can help people to connect with you.

If they do get the free item that you've offered them, they might feel more of an obligation to find out more about the rest of your products. So, you can use the free products to remind potential prospects of your other offers. The freebies can even be used as teasers to give people a taste of a larger product and that will entice them with both desire and guilt.

Stir their curiosity

One of the biggest drives that most people have is simple curiosity. It's what makes people seek out new inventions and new adventures. If we didn't have curiosity our culture would stagnate and we'd never have discovered fire or learned how to cook and create recipes. Finding out what happens next when you do something is a very strong motivator for the human species, and it can be used to help you sell your products. All you have to do is put yourself in the position of the buyer and then try to figure out how to tease them into wanting to know more.

The strategic plan

The biggest question in your prospective buyer's mind may be: "Just exactly what is this new product like?" As simple as that may sound, the drive behind that would be curiosity. It's like when you are sitting at a restaurant and you are looking at the menu, trying to make a choice of what to buy. Your inclination is to read the descriptions and become curious about one dish versus another. You may even decide to ask the waitress what the dish is like before you order. Similarly, most people want to have some idea of what the product they are deciding upon is like to experience.

In face-to-face selling, answering that question is easy. You pull out a sample or the actual product and let them try it out. Voila! Instant sale. But, online the curiosity itself has to be used to get the potential customer to imagine what it would be like to experience this product. Or you get them so worked up about finding out for themselves what it's like that they are willing to put their money down to order it just to answer that question for themselves.

So, basically you can either choose to leave the product somewhat mysterious and by nature of what you don't say, sell that product with a trigger of curiosity. Or, you can choose to give exquisite detail of what the product is like with the caveat that the buyer must experience it for themselves to really understand how wonderful the experience really is. In other words, you will constantly allude to the experience with descriptive, powerful, copy without actually making it easy for the mind to grasp. It's always slightly out of focus.

Your copy should also have a similar style even if you decide to focus on a story or stop just short of revealing the secret that you were going to share to your readers unless they buy your product.

And, there are many ways to keep people engaged using a style that triggers curiosity by using phrases like, "wait, there's more..." or "If you think this is interesting, wait until I what I have to say now..." These types of phrases pull the reader deep into the copy and stir the curiosity to get to the point of the sales page or product.

The psychological triggers

If you ever remember being enchanted by bedtime stories as a youngster, you know that you couldn't wait to know what happened to the hero or heroine at the end of the story. Once you're involved in a story, no matter what it is, you want to know how it ends.

On the other hand, if you tell the reader too much too soon, the story loses its charm. There's no more sense of mystery or excitement. Anything that is too quick to reveal its charm come off as a desperate attempt to seduce the reader in a cheap and trashy way. Often, it turns people off instead of turning them on. However, if you can leave just a little of that story untold and bring the reader in by holding back, then you will find that they have a much higher interest level in the product you offer. So, even though the product hasn't changed, you have triggered a psychological element in the person reviewing the offer that values something that isn't so quick to give itself away.

That's because people value things that are exotic, mysterious, and slightly out of reach. If it is available to everyone and easy too, then people tend to value it less. It devalues itself by making itself appear common, instead of intriguing. So, adding an air of mystery or making something just slightly out of reach can be a great way to not only stir your potential customers' curiosity but also bring up the estimation of value for your product.

How to implement effectively

If you are selling products that have intellectual property rights like books, then you have a perfect market for this particular strategy. That's because what you are selling lends itself quite well to disclosing only some information, but not all of it. That's reserved for people who buy your product.

If you take a look at Amazon.com, they know how to use this strategy to sell their books online. They let you take a "peek" inside the book and show you the table of contents and a sample chapter, sometimes. This is a great way to stir the reader's curiosity, particularly if the chapter ends at a point where it's begging you to buy the book to find out what happens next.

While Amazon's strategy takes a bit of technical know-how, you can do the same with your sales pages. You can give just enough information to the reader to stir their curiosity and then make the offer to have them buy the eBook that you are selling to satisfy their curiosity.

You can also use this strategy on your sales pages. You would tell the reader that you are going to reveal a benefit or payoff somewhere in the sales page that will really be of value to the reader. They will be encouraged to read the entire sales page just to find out the secret that you've hidden in there somewhere.

It's sort of the same strategy as when you are given a clue at the beginning of a sales letter that lets the reader in on a way to save big money on the offer, if they read the entire letter and follow the instructions hidden somewhere in the middle. Here you are telling them that if they take the time to unveil the mystery of how to get an extra discount, then they will be rewarded by saving money!

Not only are you getting people engaged in the copy this way, but you are also raising the probability that they will take the time to comprehend the offer too. That's because you will have captured there attention more and they will be more likely to pay closer attention to your offer. This can really benefit you if what you are selling needs this type of higher level comprehension.

Aside from letting the reader know that there is a secret or mystery that you are willing to unveil in the copy, you can also stir curiosity through testimonials. A testimonial is an account of someone else using the product that you're selling and how they perceived it added value to their lives. This can work very well to stir the imagination and curiosity of people online who don't have the luxury of holding a sample in their hands or downloading a demo copy.

So, say you are selling acne-fighting makeup. Of course, you can include a number of testimonials of how it cleared up the face of people in record time and how it made their face feel silky smooth and grease-less. But, an even more effective approach would be to simply have a video of someone trying it on and showing their confidence and love of life increase just because they used the product. Isn't this what most commercials do? There's the aftershave that after it's used, the man becomes a chick magnet. And, of course, it may sound unbelievable, but many men will be tempted to try the product to see if it really works as well for them.

What's important to remember though is that you don't make any statements that aren't true about your product. In the commercials that show men being swamped by women after they put on a specific aftershave, there is never a statement that suggests that the aftershave itself has the power to draw women like flies. Instead, it is alluded to and hinted at, so that potential buyers get curious as to whether it really would work for them.

Some of the questions you want floating around in the minds of your potential buyer after they read your copy are: "How would it feel for me to experience this product?" or "Will it work this way for me?" In order to get that question to float around and hook into the mind of the potential buyer, you have to leave some of the facts unsaid. You have to allude to things rather than be straightforward where the logical mind can then reject the trigger very easily. Instead, engage the emotions and the desire to experience the product for themselves.

Timing this strategy

There are various times to use this strategy depending on whether you are sowing small seeds of curiosity with leading statements that ask the reader to keep reading to unveil more of your message or whether you have one giant secret you are going to unveil somewhere in the copy.

If you are doing the hidden secret in the copy type of strategy, you need to be upfront at the very beginning of the sales page or offer that there is something hidden deep within the copy that will be of value to them. Maybe it saves them money. Maybe it gives them a free gift. Maybe it provides them with an upgrade for using a specific code. You get to decide what that benefit is and make sure the reader knows that it will be of high value to them, and then you can either tell them what it is or keep leading them into the copy to get them even more curious.

Then after you tell them at the beginning, keep your word and hide that secret benefit somewhere in the copy so that they can have the joy of discovering it for themselves and reaping the benefits.

If you are using this strategy in small bite-sized chunks, then you might spread out small phrases like: "Wait until you hear what comes next..." This will make people keep reading the copy even though no specific benefit has been claimed for reading the next part of the copy. It's just an instrument to stir curiosity. In cases like that, you will do this every so often down the copy of the sales page. It should be interspersed throughout the copy in regular intervals to lead the reader through the copy with a sense of expectation and anticipation characteristic of the state of curiosity.

Lastly, if you are using the strategy of alluding to some experience that the reader must have for themselves, you will want to create a story of a first-hand experience, either through words or a video, without actually saying what benefit they will get from it. Instead, allude to some experience that just has to be seen for themselves to get the full impact and for that they need to buy the product. Then, you will want the entire sales page or promotion to be all about these allusions and then make sure at the end they know where to order the product that will satisfy their curiosity.

Embrace simplicity

It can be a lot harder to write copy that is simple and easily understandable than it is to write complex copy. But, the rewards are worth it. You appeal to a need in most people to be met at their own level. If you talk down to them in tone, they will perceive the copy as condescending and lose interest. If you make it an exercise in grammar school reading, they will also feel slightly insulted or unappreciative. To connect with your buyers, you have to learn to meet them exactly where they are, by embracing a simplicity that appeals to both educated and non-educated alike. And, obviously, that can be a bit of a challenge.

The strategic plan

When you use simplicity as your strategy, you don't just pay attention to the words and tone of your copy, you also have to realize that the marketing offer should be reduced to its simplest elements. You are reaching out to people on a level that feels comfortable to them, and you are also going to make it very easy for them to heed your call to action to buy your product.

If you have words that are too high brow in the copy, odds are you will impress the professors who come across your ad, but turn off the average Joe who just wants to know what you're talking about. So, keeping the words simple, while the content of the conversation in an adult format, can help you reach a wider audience and promote your products better.

In addition, you want to take a close look at the offer you are making. Is there anything about it that can confuse the potential buyer? Is there information in it that you need a specific degree to read? The only time you want to get so excessively technical is when your target audience is a grouping of technically talented people. Otherwise, seek to make the product and its features easy to understand and appreciate.

Some Internet marketers make the mistake of making the offers themselves complicated by asking for one payment now, and then a different payment later – for the same product! So, for instance, they might say that to sign up for membership on a site is $25.00 setup fee, plus a $15/month subscription fee. While it may seem simple, people can get quickly turned off by two different fees or subscription prices. Try to keep your pricing standard so that when an upgrade is requested, the customer knows what they're paying for.

Sometimes the way a product works can be complicated. An example of this is cosmetic treatments like teeth whitening or acne- fighting programs that need customers to follow specific directions to obtain maximum results. While there may not be much you can do to change the number of days of treatment, the steps they need to take with each treatment, and sometimes the products they need to buy for different types of complexions and body types, you can try to simplify those instructions as much as possible.

For instance, in the case of acne-fighting programs, you might want to educate the customer that it takes "3 steps" to follow the regime correctly. Then, talk about the astringent, the blemish cream, and the moisturizing toner separately under each step. This leaves them thinking, "Oh, just three steps." Instead of the opposite reaction which would trigger panic at the complexity of the entire program.

In the same way, if you have the option to overwhelm your customers with choices or to offer a clear and simple choice, choose the simple one. Once a person buys into your featured product they may then be more interested in seeing the full line of products you have to offer later.

The psychological triggers

People are generally lazy and/or lead very complicated lives that make them relish the opportunity to pick up something much simpler. Either way, people deeply appreciate the simplicity of offers that don't take too much effort to understand or overwhelm them with choices they don't have time to make. They would rather have someone else do the hard work for them and then they come in and just be able to sign on the dotted line.

If you think about our modern day culture, this appreciation of simplicity grows more and more as our lives become overburdened with people trying to steal our time and attention everywhere we go. We'd rather not have to pay too close attention to anyone or anything that doesn't make our lives easier, because honestly, they are already seem to be careening out of control!

In particular, the demographic that most appreciates simplicity are parents of small children who are working full-time and/or care giving for others. Even though they may really need a product that simplifies their lives, they may not have time to investigate it. Or, if they are out shopping for themselves, they may give themselves less time and attention than they do to their growing families. In situations like that, you only have a few minutes to capture their attention and sell them on a product.

You see many more of these people who live hurried and time- crunched lives appearing on the Internet than ever before. They don't have the time to go retail shopping and find that Internet shopping saves them time and money. But, just because that's true doesn't mean that they're willing to wade through your complicated offer just to buy your product. On the contrary! They want things to be so simple that you've made up their mind for them, even before they've showed up at your site. They want your offers to show that you've done the research and legwork that is necessary to identify quality products and that you are willing to sell it to them in an easy and fast way online!

If you can deliver that type of offer to them, they are highly motivated to make the purchase right then and there so they can get onto other things that need their attention.

How to implement effectively

To implement this strategy review your copy to make sure it is easily understood. It shouldn't contain large or complicated words, but not read too childishly either. You can make those words sing by using stories, bullet points, or emotional cues to draw your reader in. It's not so much the words you use, but what you are saying with those words that will sell the product for you.

And, of course, the content needs to be sure to be as uncomplicated as possible. Even if your product requires some series of steps to produce results, you will want to sum it up as quickly and briefly as possible to get the message across. Don't try to make the reader have to figure out what your product is all about. It should be self- explanatory from your copy what it is about and why the person should buy it. When you list your benefits, they should be easy enough to understand and appreciate that they need no further explanation or selling.

Finally, a very simple strategy for new potential buyers is to isolate one choice for them in a lineup of products that you've selected as the best choice for your particular demographic. You should be able to feature that item on your website and explain why this product is the one product they need to buy, after visiting your site. Always pick one, very high quality, good value item to promote to your new customers and then tell them all the benefits in simple, easy to read, language. When a person is browsing with little time to review all your lineup, they will appreciate the fact that you've picked the very best item for them to buy without much hassle having to think about it.

Sure, you may have any number of other products on your site, but if you know your visitors and their tastes, then they are relying on you to make their shopping experience as simple as if they had a virtual shopping assistant. They will want you to bring to their attention the best deal that they can get for the types of products that they are looking for.

You should make the offer as simple as possible too. Online, that means you want to give them the option to pay instantaneously using credit cards or even PayPal. They should know that when they click the button to buy, they will be making an order that will be delivered promptly to their home. If you are selling virtual products, you can easily deliver it instantaneously to their computer, and add an element of instant gratification to the sale too.

When you choose a product to feature and the customer is a new customer, you should also make it easy for them to sign up to buy. Nothing deters more customers than a complicated sign-up form that asks for addresses or other information that is not relevant to the sale. All you really need to market to anyone online is a valid email, so choose to keep your registration forms simple and collect only what's necessary to close the sale. Your customers will appreciate that and tend to trust you more.

If you don't know what offers people want, why not ask them? You can set up a simple survey that gives them a coupon or other freebie for participating. It will help you to define the best offers to put forward to your visitors and helps them appreciate the fact that you're listening. Just keep the survey as simple as possible with radio buttons they can click to select and option out of various other options and then give them their freebie immediately after they complete the survey. If it is a coupon for one of your products, you've not only gotten valuable feedback, but you've also motivated them to make a purchase before the coupon expires.

Always have a great introductory offer for new customers, which gives them exactly what they need to leave your site feeling satisfied. Once they get something that meets their needs and you chose it, they are more apt to trust your opinion more when they visit later. By then you will know that they might be interested in other products in your lineup that are not featured or introductory offers.

Timing this strategy

As suggested earlier, this strategy is best used when you are first introducing yourself to new customers. You want to meet new customers at their level and go the extra mile to make their lives easier. You can do this by taking the hassle out of the shopping experience and guiding them to a great choice for them. They will appreciate the fact that you have made their lives easier and that the shopping experience was hassle-free.

You can always use the strategy in your copy on the sales page when you list your benefits too. The easier and clearer you message of benefits is, the more likely that someone will be able to scan them quickly and make up their mind instantly. You can even reinforce the idea of simplicity through the layout of your copy.

You can use bullets and bolding to pick out the relevant words that people can scan on a busy day in the office as they are browsing your site. Maybe they don't want to take the time to read all the copy, but you've made it simple enough for them to get the message they need by isolating the relevant words and information that they can spot quickly by scanning the web page. Then, when they see something that intrigues them more, they can choose whether to read the normal text or not next to it. Either way, this is more in line with today's hectic work schedules and multitasking lives. The easier you make it for someone to get your message and make a choice, the more likelihood they will appreciate you and your products more.

Harmonize to mutual agreements

If you've ever seen two old married people mimic each other due to having been together for so long, you'll have some idea of how this strategy works. You want to be able to harmonize with your potential buyer in such a way that they believe they've known you all their lives and are in complete agreement with everything you say. That way, when it comes time to buy the product, they will be willing to continue this fine partnership by buying your product.

When someone comes across as agreeable, it's mostly because we are seeing traits in them that we like about ourselves. Think of your circle of friends. They are your friends because they harmonize with you. You trust their opinions. You tend to agree with their point of views. You will go a little further to help a friend than you will a total stranger, in most cases. And, you do it because you know they would do the same for you if the situation were reversed. That's what a mutually beneficial friendship is like. It provides a connection of trust and mutuality that cements the relationship.

If you are in marketing, you also want to establish a relationship with your potential buyer, and it's not too different than a trusted friendship. Once you get someone to like you and identify with you, it becomes easier for them to agree with what you are saying. If what you are saying has something to do with a product you are selling, it makes the sale that much easier to achieve.

The strategic plan

What do you do when you want to make friends? You typically try to agree with people, wear the clothing they like, and compliment them. You make yourself generally non-threatening and likable. It's no different for Internet marketing. You will want to present an online image that is likable and also complements the demographic that is coming to visit your site.

Some of the most common ways to be likable is to appeal to generic values of honesty or integrity. In particular, if you are marketing on social networks, you will want to focus on authenticity so that people feel comfortable with you. That means that the image that you present online should match the person you are offline. If later, someone finds out you are not who you say you are, that will be the end of those relationships and in social sites, news like that spreads instantly and can be quite damaging. So, stay on the safe side and present an authentic and honest image and you will be respected and liked for that.

You can influence people to harmonize with you through some subtle subconscious cues too. For instance, if you say something positive and ask the other person to agree with you (and, they most likely would), then you have started harmonizing with the possible be buyer. This can be something as simple as saying: "Lovely day, don't you think?" While it may seem a courtesy, it's actually a very subtle way of beginning the slide down the path of total agreement and mutual trust.

While you are not standing face-to-face with your customers online, you can use the same strategy by using many of the same phrases that will illicit agreement from your visitor. It will have to be something that most people would have a difficult time replying "no" to, otherwise, the first no in their minds is what breaks the spell. You want very innocuous phrases that are tied to statements that are generally positive and produce agreement on the part of the person reading them.

Besides these subtle verbal clues, you can actually make a person agree with you through mirroring their behavior. Although this works best in face-to-face encounters, the strategy can be implemented online in group forums, and social networking sites. So, we'll discuss it next.

The psychological triggers

Infants learn how to mimic their parents and that's how they learn many of their own behaviors. In general, when we don't know how to act in a particular situation, we have been taught to look to others to gain wisdom from the experience of others. Those people we look up to, we also emulate, and this is also a form of mirroring. So, there are basically two foundational behaviors associated with mirroring: learning and socializing.

If you are sitting in front of a new product now, part of what you need to do to make a decision is to learn about it. If you've already got an agreeable authority on the product in front of you (the salesperson), then the likelihood that you will use their knowledge to help make a decision is very likely. But, if you really want to trust this person, they have to be likable. So, the fact that they start to mirror you or lead you into an agreeable frame of mind, will help you make up your mind on whether to close the sale or not.

So, this strategy is used both by the sales person to create a degree of familiarity with the potential customer, and it can also be used to mimic more successful sales professionals by mirroring their actions. It's not just a strategy that works on customers, but it can also be used consciously to create a learning environment for the Internet marketer too. It's always easier to learn something by following proven methods that others have tried and tested, rather than learning everything on your own the hard way.

So, when you do find someone worth emulating, take the time to understand not only the keywords and phrases important for the interaction, but how to handle the environment too. All great modeling comes with a specific environment for learning. Just like people don't learn how to play tennis on a golf course, you don't learn how to implement Internet marketing techniques in a retail store. Go to the experts that are already using these techniques in the specific environment where they should be used. Then, try out the same techniques in the same environment.

That means that you aren't just seeking to emulate a specific person on the Internet who has proven successful with a specific technique. Also take a look at the environment they've established to generate the sales and mimic that as best as you can with your websites and sales pages. That way, you will create a perfect mirroring of their techniques and ambiance.

How to implement effectively

Another word for the mirroring associated with this strategy is also called patterning. In patterning, we are going to try to create mutual agreement through harmonizing consciously with the sales prospect in front of us. For instance, if a person sits down and crosses their feet towards you, you might do the same. If they have a cup of coffee, you would get one too and join them. In this way, you are saying non-verbally to your sales prospect: "I agree with you." And, that translates into the other person thinking: "Gee, this person sure is agreeable."

If you are in social groups online and you are marketing with comments and a backlink to your URL, it pays to be courteous and agreeable. Don't flame other people and in general, choose to agree rather than disagree. You can easily set up reciprocity of good feelings by complimenting the poster or genuinely stating how you agree with the post. Then, add your backlink to your website show other thoughts on the matter that people might be interested in reading. This is one way to drive traffic to your site and get more people viewing your online offers.

Even though you can't solicit a response back from your online visitor, you can still ask some rhetorical questions that lead to agreement. They would be more like the following:

Ninety-five percent of people made three times their money on this investment. Wouldn't you like to be one of those people?

Suffering from allergies makes people miserable. Wouldn't it be nice to know you could go out in the spring and fall and breathe easily? Taking care of pets is important, if we want them to be around a long time. And, wouldn't you want your cat/dog to be healthy and live a long life?

All of these types of rhetorical questions will lead to agreement because they appeal to your readers in ways that are subtle but true. It would take a real contrary person to disagree that they didn't want to make money or stop suffering from allergies. And, if someone is on a pet site that you own, odds are they love their pets and want them to live long and healthy lives. So, if you know the demographic you are attracting, you can generally think up some very easy non- threatening phrases to insert into your web copy that will harmonize with your readership. Once they start harmonizing, it won't be long before you can insert: "And, wouldn't buying this product solve all your problems?" By the time they get to that phrase, they've already been saying, yes, yes, yes, that another yes is due to come out unbidden.

Next, you want to locate people online who are marketing the goods and services that you want to market. These are typically your competitors, although it can be successful affiliates or other Internet marketers who are coaching you. You will want to establish the same attitude and confidence in your products and services that they have with theirs. You want to get into their mindset and use that to help you write copy that sounds similar to their copy, in tone and content.

Remember that you can't just plagiarize other people's online content. Always seek to add your own, although you can paraphrase and keep the gist of what is being said, as long as you don't plagiarize. In some cases, you can even give credit to people and amp up your credibility and aura of success by associating with partners who are willing for you to use their name and words, as long as you credit them. Then, it makes it very simple to emulate someone who is coaching you, if they are also willing to let you use their words online.

If you have such a program available to you, you can sign up and try to get a hold of any books, articles, or information packets that can help you develop a similar pattern of success with their ideas on marketing. Even if the program isn't specific to your market, there are many Internet marketing gurus that have plenty of valuable advice on how to shift your sales upwards and they all deserve an ear now and then. Just choose a couple that you want to pattern and then immerse yourself in their programs and products to understand how they got to be as successful as they did. Then, just mimic those techniques and you have an easy way to get started on the road to Internet marketing riches much faster than if you just did things by trial and error.

Timing this strategy

The timing for this strategy is at the beginning, in the middle, and near the end. At the beginning, you are trying to establish rapport with your sales prospect by finding innocuous ways to connect and harmonize with the other person. In face-to-face interactions this might mean having a cup of coffee with them or chatting briefly about their favorite sports team. Online it would be to project an agreeable image that resonates with your demographic.

Next, you would want to start peppering your copy with rhetorical questions that lead the reader into agreement with you more and more. These should be non-threatening and evoke and emotional response.

Finally, in your call to action, you will ask for the sale by using another leading question that also seeks agreement. It's the final bold move that if timed right will have your prospect quickly reaching to click on the buy button on your sales page.

And, of course, you can use this strategy for your own education by learning how to mimic and pattern yourself off other people's successful sites and strategies. Take what you learn and apply it in the same environment that they implemented it within and that way your tram ride up the mountain of success becomes that much easier.

Put your money where your mouth is

Consumers these days are very smart. They are hypersensitive to marketing gimmicks and paranoid about being conned with slick advertisements. This generation grew up with television and the commercial advertisements that literally ruled the marketplace and human behavior. In doing so, they became inoculated to many of the psychological triggers that were a bit underhanded, but powerful non-the-less. They also can spot a con a mile away, so you have to be extra careful to be as honest and forthright as possible. The payback though is that if you are squeaky clean honest, not just with the good features of your products but the bad ones too, people will tend to value your opinions as a marketer more. You will trigger a deep psychological appreciation of your honest behavior in a sea of dishonest merchandisers. That's why honesty has to be one of the top psychological triggers to implement when you are doing any type of marketing, online or otherwise.

The strategic plan

Honesty is similar to authenticity, except it is a tad more straightforward. You can be authentic about who you are and still misrepresent the products you sell based on your spotless image of personal integrity. Honesty, in this case, is to be truthful – plain and simple. We aren't talking about the truth that you would like to believe, it is about the truth of what the consumer would like to hear. For that, you need to have their best interest at heart, and that's the role of honesty in your life. You have to take into account that even though selling is about making money, if you sell something that ultimately dupes the consumer in any way, it will come back to bite you in the butt in the end. It may take a while, but it will come back eventually. In today's social networking climate, the payback may be sooner than you think.

Social networking sites are great sites to establish a presence and start cultivating a bigger contact list. You build a circle of friends that trust you and will listen to your status updates and newsfeeds. You develop more connections in groups. All these interactions need to have a degree of authenticity and honesty. When you post a link back to your site, you want to be sure it leads to an honest way of doing business. Otherwise, the first person on the network that gets scammed will send out a general message to all their friends to avoid you, and then those friends will turn around and do the same. Once your reputation as an honest person is lost on a social networking site, most of your marketing opportunities are gone too. This is particularly true if you seek to increase the number of friends in your list solely to market them.

There are instances when people send messages or post updates that are viewable by all their friends that certain people are "spammers" and not to accept them as friends. That's all it takes to get you silently blacklisted even if your account remains current with the host site. So, always seek to add value and bring an honest level of interaction to social networking sites in particular.

When you recommend a product, your product or some-one else's, be sure they understand the relationship you have with the vendor, what you think of it in detail, and let them know if you are an expert or not. If the product has faults, don't shove them under the rug. It's more than likely the consumers will pick up on those faults as objections and if you leave them unaddressed you've lost the sale. So, always address the faults and either reframe them or make them insignificant. If the fault is major, just don't sell that product. The choice is yours.

The psychological triggers

If you are honest with your sales presentation, people begin to open up more to the possibility of buying from you. It can also be a point of differentiation between you and your competitor. Have they dealt with them and found them less than honest? That's why they should buy from you instead! Honesty is something that is hard to come by and easy to lose. It has to be earned by a continual willingness to put the other person's interest before your own.

People understand the great motivation to lie: self-gain. Lying in this day and age is rampant, from politicians to lovers.

People lie to get their way. Just like when you were little and your parents asked you: "Did you do your homework?" And, you lied to get out of having to do it. If our parents weren't particularly invested in teaching us the principle of honesty, that also came across. Like when they said, "Do as I say, not as I do." That basically told you it was okay to lie about your values because it was just a standard used to get other people to do what you wanted them to do. Otherwise, they would have taken the trouble to match their actions where their words went. They would have put their money where their mouth went instead of giving you a mixed message that it's okay to say one thing and do another.

So then when you lie to others you learn that it generally lets you off the hook. You don't have to explain that you really didn't feel like doing your homework or that the product you are selling has faults. That way, if no one objects or tries to verify your story, your lie eases the way to get your way without much effort on your part to be honest about anything. So, it's also a form of laziness. That lack of effort though does come across to people eventually as they do more business with you. They begin to realize that you are the type of person who only does what's in your own best interest and once that message gets through, people pull away in disgust. You become completely untrustworthy. Anything you say after that is suspect. So, while honesty is easy to establish and maintain with a little effort, once you lose it, you lose the necessary trust to continue with the relationship, whether it is personal or business.

And how does all this happen? Here you will be surprised to find out that this interaction on a psychological basis is completely NON- VERBAL. That's right! You may think you have to speak to tell a lie, but your actions are shouting it out loud and clear to your customers. It doesn't even have to be a black and white lie because people are sensitive to being lied to and conned. They will pick up the non-verbal cues of your behavior and add two and two together to figure out that you are not trustworthy. They won't even bother confronting you because, after all, if you are a liar you will deny it. If you are being truthful, you'll deny it. So, they will simply watch your behavior and make a judgment of you and then take their business elsewhere if they decide you aren't trustworthy. Now, though, they may also decide to tell all their friends too before they go.

So, to be perceived as an honest person takes more than just telling the truth. It takes putting someone else's interest above your own, specifically your customer's needs! It also takes a cultivation of behaviors that trigger the association of honesty in your customer's mind. Some of these we'll discuss in the next section.

How to implement effectively

One of the behaviors that suggests a "cover-up" is when you have a website with too many glitzy images and flashing neon fonts. While it may be a way of attracting attention, it also gives off the aura of intentional distraction, like you don't want someone to notice that the product isn't what it is. That's why some social networking sites like Facebook have very clean, crisp, profile images with little extraneous hype or cluttered appearances. This is often referred to as a "professional" appearance and with that moniker comes the suggestion that you are a person of integrity that does an honest business.

So, when you set up your websites, endeavor to portray an honest image versus one of an over-commercialized hyped up sales image that screams "smoke and mirrors." The result will be that the people coming to your site will trust you more because you've kept your profile and site clean, crisp, understandable, and thus it triggers the idea that you are a professional, honest, person.

Next, you want to be sure that products you sell are exactly what you say they are and no less. This goes even for the affiliate offers that you put up. If you associate with dishonest affiliates that reputation comes back to you and can lose you customers. So, you want to investigate your sales affiliates and make sure that they are on the up and up. You should use a redirect page for each affiliate in the event you need to pull an offer because one of your customer complains of dishonest practices. This way, you can change one redirect page and keep all the links on your website still pointing to that page. This is the quickest way to keep control of the affiliates you advertise without having to search through each web page in your site for where you've added a particular affiliate link. And, it keeps your site honest when you can pull bad offers at the first whiff of trouble.

Make sure your copy doesn't have any small white lies or outright exaggerations. While it may seem unnoticeable to you, people pick up on these very quickly and it can discredit the rest of your offer.

The same is true of your affiliate offers. Make sure they are selling exactly what they say they are selling in the copy.

If you have a product that you think is good, but has an obvious flaw, just be sure to let your customers know the flaw exists. You can use marketing strategies to minimize or reframe the flaw, but definitely mention it. If you don't mention it, the customer will figure it out and keep it as an unaddressed objection in their mind that will kill the sale every time. It's much better to be forthright about the flaws than to ignore them all together.

If you're not sure how the copy reads, why not test it out on someone. Just ask them to read the copy and tell you what they think the ad is really saying. You can even try this approach and use a white lie or exaggeration and see how easily people pick up the deception! If you want to portray an image of honesty, there's no real way to do it other than having some integrity.

Timing this strategy

You have to be honest in all your dealings, not just in the presentation of your website and copy. If you promise to have things delivered within 72 hours, than do everything in your power to keep that promise. Don't try to get orders by lying or it will end up making you look bad in the end. If you run out of a product and need to substitute with another, make sure the customer knows and agrees before you send it out, or provide them a refund.

It's almost always better to provide a refund with no questions asked, even if the person is dishonest and used the product. The reason for this is that a dishonest person will likely try to ruin your reputation, if they don't get their money back. An honest person will deserve the money back, typically. So, in terms of customer service, always make the customer happy regardless whether they are honest or dishonest. On the other hand, you yourself need to be a paragon of honesty to maintain your business reputation.

Blend in with the marketplace

The success of a chameleon depends on its ability to blend in with its environment to escape detection. This strategy is similar in that you want to blend in with the marketplace, not to avoid detection though, but to enhance the probability that your offering will be accepted as a natural part of that environment.

What you really want to do is always take account the needs of the marketplace before you spend too much effort trying to sell a product that has no market. Once you understand what the market prefers, you should try to generate an offer that harmonizes with that need, instead of ignoring it or going off on some new tangent all together.

So, while many life coaches will tell you to follow your dreams, your dreams are limited by the environment in which you find yourself. You can't sell as many copies of a book on crocheting as you can on finances. That's because the market is hungry for good financing information on only a few people crochet these days. So, the environment is rich for growing finance book sales but it is poor for growing crochet books. Even if you are an expert in crochet stitches, what good does it do to spend your time creating a book few other people will pay to read? Instead, focus on what the market wants and after you've sold enough to raise the capital for the crochet book, then write the book – if it still interests you.

The strategic plan

This strategy is like how you pick a career in life. In that case, the career would be your product and the environment is the job marketplace. Maybe you want to grow up to be a mime, but no one is hiring mimes. So, instead, you focus on a career that can pay you so that you can be a mime on your off hours. Maybe you become a computer technician who does shows on weekends at the local mall. When you make enough money as a computer technician, then you can decide whether to take the mime gig full time and make a go of it.

There is a little twist here though. You aren't just going to pick any career to make money. You're going to pick one that is similar to your actual goal. So, if your real ambition is to be a mime, you get a degree in technical theater. That way, you get to work in the environment conducive to acting and you get to be around people who love to act. Then, you can start to see if there is a way to make money as a mime too. That is the smart way to follow your dreams AND make enough money to live on.

In marketing terms, you may want to sell indoor table top atriums, but your research shows there is no market for them – don't create a website devoted solely to them then! You instead look for a market that is similar and use that to launch your sites. For instance, you may find that people are learning how to grow vegetable and flower gardens in tight economic times. Then, you would devote your site to gardening and have the atriums as one potential product that can be bought off the site.

Always seek to harmonize with the marketplace. If you are trying to sell woman's wigs, don't try to sell them in an environment that won't appreciate them – like in beauty shops where people are paid to cut your hair. Instead, you would seek out cancer groups to advertise and places where people appreciate a fine woman's wig. This is blending into your environment and is important even when you are just commenting on someone else's blog and linking back to your site from there.

The psychological triggers

Have you ever seen anyone walk in with a tie that clashes with the rest of their suit? How about when someone says something totally inappropriate for a conversation? Doesn't that just jar people into silence and staring? It's an immediate turn-off and people will often mock things that are out of place. This is how people will perceive a product that is not timed to harmonize with the marketplace.

Even in the West where the culture of individuality reigns, you will see a look of disgust come across people's faces when something is distinctly out of place or interrupts the flow of an event. That's because our culture works on unwritten rules of social cooperation that are meant to help people work together in harmony, even when everyone is their own individual. There are still social rules in place that people follow to make everyone comfortable and to ease the social underpinnings of a civil society.

When people fall outside those rules, it triggers a social consciousness that degrades the value of that interaction. You are speaking out of turn. You are not following the rules. You are creating disorder in their lives, and they won't appreciate it. More than likely they will either openly mock someone for stepping out of line or they will ignore it completely. Either way, a product that isn't in harmony with its environment is going to receive a very poor public reception, unless that public has been primed for the introduction of a product that steps outside the norms.

If, however, you have a product that falls into the market at just the right time, the public is ready to accept it and the probability that you will close more sales is much higher. So, you want to check what the social environment is like before you devote much of your Internet marketing resources to a product or market that just doesn't have enough juice to justify the effort. It will make your life easier in the long run to go with the flow than it will be to try to fight it.

Then, once you make a bit of money on the markets that are already selling and you still have the desire to try something different – go for it! You will have learned much more about what your market wants, how to play on those desires, and how to make money online selling similar products.

How to implement effectively

To implement this strategy you have to do your homework. Research the marketplace in depth before you commit money, time, and resources to an online sales venture that is doomed to fail because you didn't do this one thing: Harmonize with the marketing environment. With new products, this is even more important because it will have to still meet the needs of the market to sell and you may have fewer ways to determine how it will be received without proper researching consumer trends.

One way to test the environment for a new product is to do a trial offer and see how many people bite. This can be in the form of a popup window or limited time offer. The number of sales on that product will give you an idea of how many people would actually buy the product if you did a full sales page and promotion for it. If it has trouble selling, you can lower the price and try the ad again to see if the price range was off. If it still has trouble selling or even generating interest, odds are the market is not ready for this product or simply can't appreciate it because it is too different.

Another way you can get products to harmonize with the environment is to offer accessories with it that the market loves. Take for instance, cell phones. They were rather new and at first all they did was call people's numbers remotely. Now, they offer cameras, voicemail, special ring tones, web access, and even games. All those people who never had a need to call people from outside their home suddenly found the features appealing to the electronic gizmo culture of our times. Now, everyone carries a cell phone and the more features your phone has the more status it carries.

Maybe you are selling cosmetics online, and so you pair it with some pretty purses or bags. Now you've got two markets: people who wear make-up and people who love to get new purses every season. You've accessorized your offering so that it fits into multiple environments.

You can even just change the marketing perception of an old product to make it fit into a new culture. That's a way of upgrading the image of something that people consider an old-fashioned or traditional and making it appeal to modern tastes. This is one way to get old products to blend into new environments by offering them a new slant.

The diamond ring is an excellent example of this strategy to harmonize with the new environment where people didn't want just a solitaire diamond like everyone else had. They wanted something different. So the diamond industry took their diamond rings and created new concepts so that diamond rings would still be marketable in a changing environment. They started creating right- hand rings for women who were happy being single, but wanted to show off their wealth. They created bands with multiple diamonds and called them eternity rings to celebrate anniversaries. They generally upgraded the old-fashioned concept of a single stone ring to one that was more luxurious and could express a greater degree of individuality for people in our times, whether married or not. And diamond sales went up dramatically because they now had a wider market since they had learned to blend in seamlessly to the new culture of individuality, affluence, and even single people.

You can take the example of the diamond industry and apply it to your own products. What can you do to make your products blend in more with today's fashions, tastes, and cultural biases? Maybe it just means offering products in a variety of colors. Maybe you want to add some accessories like a pouch for a cell phone, if you are selling purses. Maybe you want to remove some items from your inventory or their accessories that stamp your products as being out of step with the times. You don't want to be the person selling typewriters when the entire market was going to computer word processors. It just doesn't make good business sense. Instead, read the signs of the times and unload your inventory and get into something the marketplace wants and appreciates.

Timing this strategy

The timing for this strategy refers more to a cultural sense of time. You want to be take note of what's going on in your society and try to keep ahead of trends happening in your market niches. You want to use that knowledge to predict what might be a good seller and what isn't worth your time marketing. So, much of this strategy is done even before you build a website or offer a product in your inventory. Once it's up there, the only choice you have is to either unload it or accessorize it to get it to match.

You can keep the news of what's happening in the niches you are interested in by subscribing to trade blogs or journals. You should read the latest of what's happening in your world and always attempt to do a trial run for products which may seem like a good

Idea, but you can't locate relevant research to back up that sentiment. So, test it out. Then, the marketplace can tell you whether it's a potential winner or a dud without spending too much time and effort getting an entire campaign up and running.

Exact the facts

Ever hear speeches on a presidential campaign? Many of them are full of rhetoric but short on facts. The reason for that is they try to engage the emotions, but when it comes time to vote, people really want the facts of where the candidates stand. The same is true when you make a buying decision. You may be attracted emotionally at first to the offer, but to close the decision to buy, you have to have a logical reason that is based on sound facts. If the Internet marketer fails to provide exact facts to close the deal, the prospective buyer may feel the offer is vague or not credible. So, it's always a good strategy to exact the facts of any offer to make it as specific and credible as possible.

The strategic plan

What's the best way to be perceived as an expert on some subject? Having the facts about your subject makes you an authority in the eyes of other. With authority comes credibility and with credibility comes trust. And, trust is a major component of any business transaction. When people trust a vendor they are more willing to purchase from them. They have confidence in the products that the vendor sells because they trust the vendor. So, when you seek to be more specific with the facts of your sales presentation, then you invoke an air of expertise and authority. That eventually winds down to more sales, if you can convince people that you really do know what you are talking about more than others.

This strategy works on the facts that you decide to write in your copy. It can be about the social facts that make your product valuable to people or it can be facts about the product itself.

Say you are selling all natural food products. You can focus on the facts that make a natural food product valuable in a conventional marketplace. For that, you would need to compare the facts of conventional products to organic products in a very specific way. You might say (if it were true), "America's conventional food supply is exposed to over 100 chemicals for each pound of food grown on our farms every month." This is very specific in the number of chemicals you can avoid by eating organic foods and the intensity of the exposure. It's extremely specific and can make you look like a very informed expert on the topic of food product safety and health.

That's the way to use this strategy when you are trying to pinpoint social facts that make your product valuable. But, there's also another way.

Say you want to concentrate on the qualities of your product instead to sell it. In the above case of organic foods, you would highlight the qualities of organic foods that make them desirable to the specific market you are targeting, in this case health conscious consumers. So, you would say instead, "In a blind taste test, organic carrots tasted better than conventional carrots 90% of the time."

Now, if you are saying something that is really not true, you will trigger the dishonesty meter of most readers. So, no fibs when you use this strategy or people who are knowledgeable will eventually come across your ad and call you on it. And, you can even get in trouble with Federal guidelines of false advertising if you end up stating facts that can't be backed up with some research somewhere.

That doesn't mean you have to start a research laboratory in your basement just to get some good facts that you can use. You can use any facts by any known experts and just quote them. If they have lots of degrees it helps your product to look very credible too. That's why when new interesting facts come out, you can see it scooped up and used by marketers everywhere to sell their products, when they apply.

The psychological triggers

People really don't trust most advertising these days, particularly if it is just generic hype. But, add a few specific facts and you will see the interest level in your readership soar. The reason for that our culture really values knowledge and expertise. Some people may read your ad and then even try to verify the facts for themselves. Others will be so astounded they take your ad and tell their friends about it to make themselves sound like experts too.

Our minds are much more trained for logical thought than for the intuitive feel of an ad that may work on our subconscious, but rarely makes its way into the conscious mind. However facts speak to the side of us that is constantly searching the environment for new and interesting information. It is easily digested and understood.

Face it, we are in the information age and many children have been born into a world of computers, iPods, televisions, and radios. Testing in school emphasizes facts and the ability to be specific and knowledgeable about certain topics like math or science. We've been programmed to believe that the only way to determine whether something has value is to use the scientific method which involves understanding and testing the facts. This social framework impacts our psychology to give the Western culture a bias that appreciates facts and specificity. The more something seems to be a scientific conclusion with highly specific facts, the more credibility we assign to it. And, for sure, it reminds us of being in a class room where the authority figure, the teacher, knew all the facts and we had to submit to that knowledge to pass the grade.

Similarly, when someone triggers this automatic deferral to authority figures they trigger a deep psychological need to follow the lead of someone else. When that happens they are much more suggestible to your advertising than when they think they have to make up their own mind. Instead, they can rely on your expertise to make up their mind for them.

You also tend to sound more certain and assured when you can rattle off facts that are very specific. It really cements the case that you know what happened and you can be trusted to give an informed opinion. It's like when you are in a court case, the person who has a better recollection of the facts comes off as more believable. If you give a faint and vague recollection of events it leads to doubts in the minds of the jury. It may seem a bit unfair, but it comes across as a person trying to dodge the truth instead of someone who is sure of themselves and the facts of the case.

If you've ever been asked by a woman if she looks fat, you know that the only right answer is no. However, if you hesitate and then say no, it's that moment of uncertainty that kills the reply. There are behaviors that make your words sound unsure and being vague is one way that portrays an image of evasiveness.

Watch a poker game sometime. The best card players have a straight face and bid in the same confident manner no matter what they hold in their hands. That attitude is what comes across the table to make their opponent believe them and to help them make any hand a winning hand. That's the attitude your copy should have too online.

How to implement effectively

The first way of implementing this strategy is to be specific about the product's qualities, without necessarily sounding scientific. As long as you are incredibly specific about what the buyer is getting, it will help them to visualize and imagine owning this thing that they can only see in virtual mode over the Internet.

For example, you are selling designer purses online and you put up an ad on your website. It should go into exquisite detail over what makes this purse special. Maybe it is made of genuine, hand-stamped, leather in a deep burgundy color. Inside, it has three pouches, one for change, another for makeup and a third for your cell phone. Maybe it has a full metal zipper opening or genuine gold accents. Only you, the marketer, knows what to tell the consumer in detail about this beautiful offer you are making. The more you tell the person who is viewing the offer, the more they will have to imagine it in their mind in greater detail. Now, even though this doesn't work on authority, it works on the bias people have to use their mental powers to imagine the product they can only view in virtual mode online. So, be specific about any feature that can help your visitors touch, feel, smell, or even hear your product in their mind's eyes.

The next way is to research the environment that makes your product valuable and use the facts you unearth to sell your products. If you are selling home security systems, you might want to review crime rates and how they are rising uncontrollably because of poor economic conditions. You can even find out what the national rise in different crimes is like a 10% increase in home burglaries nationwide and use that to sell home security systems.

On tap water filtering systems use the pollution rate of bottle water to make a case for buying a home water filtering system that works at the tap source and that's very effective. It's not hard to find this information and you can even look at your competitor's sites to see what information they've manage to unearth and use it too. You might find information on the average types of contaminants found in sample water supplies and even horrify people with how many hormones and cancer drugs are there without being able to be filtered out by the local water plant.

Next, you can also use the products own unique qualities to be exceedingly specific about the benefits a buyer will get when they purchase it. So, if we continue to use the water filtration example, we would list how many contaminants it filters out and what they are. You can say how water filtering at the tap will help reduce lead too, in case you unknowingly have lead pipes in the house.

You should also use percent's to help you make the case. So, the copy might read: This ABC filters out 72% of harmful chemicals from your drinking water. If you pick a number that isn't a multiple of five it is much more memorable and believable. Ratios are also good too to implement when you are trying to create memorable facts. So, you might say, "Nine out of 10 environmentalists agree that this water filter is the best on the market."

Timing this strategy

This strategy becomes the meat of your advertisement, should you choose to use it. It should be right smack in the middle of your sales page and list all of the scientific facts that can help someone to make up their mind. You can lead people into this sales page with emotional triggers, but once they are there you want to have all the facts ready to help them close the deal. And, those facts need to be easily picked out, easily understood, and memorable. They should be so easy to remember that they can be repeated without having to look them up. It also works well if you do this strategy in bulleted points or tables. There's something about graphs, tables, and bullet lists that make it seem very scientific and to the point. Graphs, in particular, are very visual and appeal to people who may not bother to read your copy, but are impressed with graphics. So, you should include anything in your copy that lends it a very scientific and knowledgeable air that says you've actually taken the time to research your subject. People will be impressed and will be more willing to click on the buy button.

Work up their satisfaction level

In line with the last strategy, you can use people's cultured bias towards mental engagement to create some satisfying offers.

To do that, your offers should have some level of intrigue or challenge to them, to give people a sense of accomplishment from having read them. This can take form in a suspenseful story that captures the imagination, but leaves them wondering how the story will end. If they get to the end and are surprised, that will stimulate their sense of intellectual enjoyment and increase the satisfaction level with the ad. On the other hand, if the story is as easy to predict as your choice of breakfast food each morning, then people will feel disappointed that you made it so obvious. Always leave them feeling that there was a bit of mystery or puzzle that needed to be figured out in order to get the jewel in your message.

The strategic plan

An easy and obvious sales pitch actually insults people because people get the feeling they are either being manipulated or they are being talked down to. You do want to make things somewhat easy to follow, but that doesn't mean you want to make the final point easy to predict. It's a bit of a cross between keeping things simple and being too complex to be enjoyable. It's going to have a bit of a challenge, but it shouldn't be beyond the reach of the average person to figure out.

Sometimes getting the right level of challenge in the ad can also be a challenge. Pay attention to your demographic and gear the copy to them. Then you want to speak directly to that demographic taking into account their likes and dislikes. Then, you create an offer that speaks to that level, neither above it nor below it.

Then you want to engage the reader in your copy by leading down the path that can only end in one way, the solution to an intriguing situation or puzzle. They will be so engaged with how it all works out that they will read through your entire sales copy just to see if they got it right. If it's also not obvious, they will be delighted when they get to the end and were able to figure out where you were heading. Or, they will be surprised that they didn't see the answer and be mentally stimulated by the challenge anyways. Either way, the key is to mentally stimulate them by giving them a challenge or puzzle to work on that engages different senses and ways of thinking. Even finding a new perspective from an old story can work and be mentally pleasing to many people.

The psychological triggers

The Myers-Brigg personality test is based on Jungian theory that classifies four different functions of personality: sensing, thinking, feeling, and intuition. Everyone is said to have different components of their personality that makes them use each of these components in different ways. However, the main theory says that all four of these components make up everyone's personality, even if they are utilized differently.

So, what does this have to do with this strategy? The theory can be used to help you design offers that engage people's entire brain function which will include the four components of personality. If you appeal to just the thinking function of people, obviously, the ad won't be as powerful than if you managed to appeal to three out of the four components too. People won't be stimulated enough to remember the copy or to be triggered into buying behavior. That means that you want to mentally engage people on as many levels as possible to really tie into their imagination. You want your ad not just to invoke the senses, but the thinking, feeling, and intuition part of people too.

The more components you manage to stimulate the more pleasurable the ad will be perceived. That's because the person will be stimulated more and the entire brain will be engaged in the experience of reading the ad and imagining the scenario you've invoked. The harder your brain is working the more pleasurable the entire experience is when it finally gets resolved.

Think of it as achieving a level of mastery in any hobby or activity. If you are doing something like a very easy crossword puzzle, you soon bore of the challenge and your attention drifts. Your mind needs more stimulation, and harder puzzles to get the same boost of adrenaline and accomplishment that you had when a previous level was your challenge. As long as the answers are slightly out of your reach, the puzzles remain interesting and stimulating. Eventually, when you complete the entire puzzle you have a really good feeling of accomplishment because you know it took some time and effort to get those results.

How to implement effectively

The copy that you write should appeal to people in this manner. It should be slightly challenging, enough to keep the reader's attention. This can be done through keeping a sense of suspense and mystery until the very end. A surprise ending is also very good to give a person a mental release that is pleasurable. You can even challenge the reader to see if they can figure out what the result is before they see it.

One way to do this is to add quizzes and surveys to your website. People love these types of interactive Internet toys. It's like working a crossword puzzle except there is no wrong answer. And, sometimes these can really work well if your product can be tied to the end result of the quiz.

For example, there are dating sites that make you take a personality test at the beginning to determine who you are most compatible with and then they match you based on the results. The test can be a little long and complicated, but it also offers the potential client a great feeling of satisfaction upon completing it. The interesting way to market this as a trigger is to offer it for free as a "free personality profile" for signing up to the site for a seven day free trial.

The seven day free trial gets extended to a paying membership if it's not canceled in time. The site collects the credit card information ahead of time and then they give out the free personality profile results. So, even though the personality test was challenging and it came back with some results, it was basically an advertisement for a dating site wrapped up in a puzzle/quiz type of wrapper.

To make it really interesting, you can even make a little script that they can plug into their website that has a link back to your site. It's like a badge that shows other people that you took a certain quiz or survey and you got a high score. IQ tests are very popular this way and people love to show off their IQ and then compare it to other people's IQ results. There are many Facebook applications that work on this strategy and if you create one of your own, it can literally bring tons of traffic to your site. If you don't have the skills, but you have a great idea, hire someone to create the application for you and then post it on Facebook. You are allowed to put links back to your site in the applications and it's a great work to market to people in social networking sites.

Some surveys do the same thing. They ask you to take a quick survey and then see how your answers compare to other people's answers. Then, at the end you see an advertisement related to the survey. It gives you a fun way to connect with your visitors and people generally feel very satisfied to have something intriguing and special on the site that stimulates them mentally.

Another way to implement this strategy is to engage the reader in a human interest story with a moral or surprise ending. Sort of like when you were a child and you were told the story of Hansel and Gretal. There's an element of suspense in the story that makes you want to find out if they get eaten or not. What happens to them after all is said and done?

Now, if one of them was wearing a particular sneaker that you were selling and it allowed them to evade the witch because it lit up at night and helped them find their way home, then you can make a case for why the story ended differently. But, you'd want to make it very surprising and a story that engages people's imaginations and all the senses.

To write copy that invokes not just the senses, but also the intuition seems difficult, but it's not. What you do is you basically leave a few things unsaid. You give enough information to set the story, to invoke the thinking and feeling functions, and you describe enough to evoke the senses. Then, to get people to start to use their intuition you leave enough unsaid that they have to place themselves in that spot and wonder: "What would I do in that situation?" It's sort of like the MacGyver series where he takes the gum he is chewing, adds some chemical in the environment and blasts his way out of a prison cell. You're not quite sure how he's going to do it until he actually makes a break for it, but you know all the pieces of the puzzle are there to be able to figure it out. So, you try to figure it out before the ending is given away.

Membership sites use this at times, especially if they are certifying sites. They will say that you can join up at a certain level if you have certain accomplishments under your belt. Obviously, it can't be an easy way to qualify or people everywhere would be certified under their program. So, they list the qualifications that people need to be accepted into the program at a particular level and be recognized as either a professional or a master or whatever. Of course, you have to pay for the privilege even though it was you doing the hard work.

What are the most engaging stories? Aren't they the ones you're not quite sure how they're going to end? Then, when they do end you are surprised and delighted? So, you can create a story for your product, it can be anything from how it was discovered or created to how someone used it to gain success in some endeavor. Some people like to go back in history to find out interesting stories that are not that well known that they can use to help create an "unbelievable but true" type of aura for their product. But, you can also just create a story out of your own imagination that really brings the reader into suspense with how it will all end.

Timing this strategy

You can use the strategy to engage the reader at the start of your relationship with a new customer by using quizzes and interactive challenges to bring the potential customer into your offers in a more enthusiastic manner. You can create applications that work with social networking sites that will bring traffic in from this site. If it works well it might even go viral and you'll have a great way to market people in social networking sites regardless of niche. If you can allow them to add the application to their profile where everyone can see it, it's a great way to introduce your website and products to a new and growing market. You can also use the strategy as the offer if you write captivating stories that have an air of mystery and suspense and end with the hero using your product to save the day.

Cozy up like family

If you've ever been to a foreign land where you didn't know a soul, didn't speak the language, and looked different to everyone on the street, you probably were quite relieved to see some business that you recognized like McDonald's sitting on a street corner. We all love exotic things – for a short period of time- but when we want to come home we want things that are familiar and comforting. This strategy is all about the longing for the familiar and learning how to cozy up to your sales prospects like family.

The strategic plan

Here is where brand names and familiar advertising that rings a bell in your memory become powerful. A brand name uses this strategy because people come to feel connected and rely on brands they are familiar with and tend to avoid those they do not know or trust. So, in essence, the brand becomes a familiar element, like family, and this generates repeat sales and a customer loyalty to that particular product.

But, how do people make a brand name that sticks in the mind of the sales prospect? Lots of money and advertising goes into developing brand names that are easy to remember, show up everywhere, and that will be recognizable and associated with a particular product or company. The strategy though is simply to expose the public to this brand name over and over and associate with the type of advertising that links certain qualities with that brand name.

For instance, when you think of Maytag you think of dependability and washers and dryers. That's because Maytag became such a household brand name and the commercials were always about the poor Maytag repair man who had nothing to do because the appliances rarely broke down. They were humorous and they also got across the fact that you can depend on a Maytag. Even though Maytag is just an arbitrary name, it became associated with a particular subset of qualities and a product to boot.

So, the way to achieve some sort of familiarity to a brand name is to constantly present them in front of people until they start to associate them with the product or advertising. This really isn't as hard as it sounds. And, on the Internet, it can be very easy to do, unlike television and radio ads which can quickly add up into a fortune.

And, you don't have to limit it to a brand name, you can also create eye-catching logos and display them everywhere you want to trigger an association with your website or products. Once people start to associate a symbol with a set of qualities and/or product, it can become a very powerful tool to create familiarity and interest no matter what the environment. That's because an image, unlike a word, bypasses the conscious mind and goes straight to the subconscious. People have images that they associate with certain qualities too and you can mine those cultural biases to associate different qualities of familiarity to your website and products.

For instance, say you are trying to sell flowers online. If you just put up images of flowers or bouquets, you will be showing your product but you won't be making your company or your brand of flowers any more familiar than your competitors. But, if you started a marketing campaign and added a logo with symbols of romance, like a heart or even a kiss, people start to feel your flowers are more familiar because everyone is impacted by these symbols subconsciously. Now, if you use that marketing campaign to tell people to send flowers to the people they love and you make up special "kissable" bouquets, then the idea that you are sharing romance and warmth with people when you send a flower bouquet is even more familiar. It's not just flowers people are sending now, they are sending love. And, what is a more traditional family value than love?

The psychological triggers

In a culture that relies on family and social bonds to survive, there are certain common bonds that create predictable familiarity with different words or characteristics. As an example, if you were to ask people to choose a number between 1 and 10, the majority will pick 7. Why is that? There is some unconscious programming that favors 7 as a random number and people find it the most familiar number to pick. They aren't going to pick numbers they don't like for the most part, and most people like and are comfortable with choosing the number 7 when asked to pick a random number.

What that means for you as a marketer is that you should be aware of these unconscious biases and seek to always use what's going to be familiar and comfortable to the potential buyer. In this case, you would create eBooks with "The Top 7 Tips To Breakthrough Profits" or "Seven Secrets To Light Up Your Love Life." Does it really matter that you can write about eight or that there are hundreds of these tips and secrets out there? Not really. You are marketing to the subconscious mind that favors the number seven.

You should be familiar with the most common choices that people make, whether it be the color that is preferred by most people or genders, and the top features that people want in specific products. That way, when you try to market a product, you can offer these choices to the customer and they will feel as if you got right into their head and picked up what made them comfortable. It will seem like you were listening to them specifically, when you just happen to know what most people find comforting.

Also, repetition is important when using this strategy because the mind takes a certain amount of repetition for it to take some bit of information and store it in long term memory. Without this repetition, you may love the marketing campaign, the product, or the brand, and really connect with it, but you will soon forget it too. As a marketer, you want to have a certain amount of repetition and exposure to be able to hook into the mind and send out the message that this is important information that needs to be stored in more long term memory.

While some marketers think that to repeat the same campaign year after year is a mistake, it all depends on how successful that campaign is. You shouldn't change an advertising campaign until the sales fall off. That's because even after the novelty of a campaign falls off, you then get into familiarity and comfort. When people are comfortable with a slogan, for instance, it becomes part of the popular culture. Like the slogan: "Got milk?" The dairy association used it to popularize the familiarity of milk and how good it is for you. They even used celebrities with milk mustaches to give it a giggle factor that reminds us of our youth. That campaign is popular and increases the demand for milk, but it also sinks deep into the popular mass consciousness.

In the campaign that asks "Where's the beef?" It was to sell hamburgers of a particular vendor. But, that slogan became so popular and comfortable with the majority of people that it also spun off many other meanings and associations as other people capitalized on its simple, yet effective message. Now, "Where's the beef?" means "Where's the substance?" or "Why am I being cheated?" And, people can ask the same question of other products and it means something totally different. It becomes that familiar a concept and slogan. Ultimately, that makes this slogan highly successful because people recognize it, knows what it refers to and how it can be applied elsewhere. It becomes a part of our modern day culture.

How to implement effectively

One of the first ways to implement this strategy is through mass Internet exposure. You will have to choose something to advertise, but many people use their domain names to link to a mass exposure campaign. It can also be your personal name, a brand name, your company name, but a web URL is memorable and gives instant access to many of your sales offers.

Picking a domain name is tricky these days because all the good ones are taken. To be a memorable domain name that rolls off the tongue it should be a one or two word phrase that also can be easily associated with what you are marketing on that website. Unfortunately, those have all been gobbled up by domain name investors. So, you are probably going to end up with at least three words in your domain name, unless you want to pay an investor for the rights to the domain they own. And, that can be a possibility since a domain name is a valuable piece of your marketing strategy.

You can check out domain names at places like GoDaddy. com and find out how to purchase them there. You will want to buy them with several different extensions like .org and .net to make sure no one attempts to squat on your name for future purposes. Once you own a good domain name that is memorable and easily associated with your products or services, the rest is easy. You just advertise that domain name where ever you go online. And, offline, you can advertise it in your letterhead, your business cards, even on the side of your car, if you're that adventurous.

If you aren't necessarily targeting the domain name, you still want to include it in your advertising in conjunction with whatever brand name, logo, or slogan you are using with this strategy. Then, you want to add it to your signature so that when you post online or send an email, people start to associate these images, words, or URL with your business. It's the small interactions that can have a large cumulative effect later down the line when they are trying to figure out who to contact for a particular solution. If your email is sitting in their inbox after having remained in contact with them over the course of some time, they will associate you with a familiar face and contact you.

That's also the reason that you should use social networking sites and be a member of multiple forums and groups. These types of interactions breed familiarity on a very intimate level over the Internet and they have the potential to reach many more people than just two or three coming into a retail store. Once people begin to associate your name and face with certain qualities, particularly friendship and familiarity, they are more apt to buy something from you or contact you when they have a need.

Timing this strategy

As stated above, you should make an effort to contact people on a regular basis so that your name, brand, logo or products don't fall off their horizon. You may find that by contacting them over a period of time, they will come to know and trust you, even if you don't make a sale every single time. What you are doing is building the relationship so that they start to associate you like family and miss you when you are gone. This can take some time and patience on your part, but the rewards are that you will be turned to when a sales opportunity does come up.

Always have some idea of what elements on your website and sales offers can trigger this association of familiarity. It can be the words you use, the images you display, or even just your name. Once people get really familiar with who you are and what you do, they become more trusting and less resistant to being marketed. So, although the strategy isn't going to reap an instant sale, it will play on the subconscious mind of your targets so that it will reap new and repeat sales very effectively.

Hope for better things to come

Everyone knows what the 2016 elections are all about: Change, safety and making the US great again. That's right because when things are bad, the only thing left to do is to hope for better things to come. For that, we know we need to change the way things are. And, even though there is no definite promise of what will change or how things will change, sometimes people pin all their hopes on something different just because the present moment is uncomfortable. It's just basic human nature and, in fact, hope is a wonderfully positive human emotion.

Hope also helps to motivate many sales too. That's because people typically are looking for solutions to problems when they buy. They aren't necessarily looking for a specific item, they are looking for something that resolves some issue and benefits them. That's why sales pages don't go into great depth on the actual product, but instead they focus on the benefits. And, this is particularly important when you are marketing on the trigger of hope. You have to sell an ideal that things will be better when a person buys your product.

The strategic plan

Since you are trying to trigger the emotion of hope in your prospective buyer, all you have to do to understand how to invoke that is to place yourself in the shoes of someone visiting your site. Maybe it is someone who is aging and unhappy at the many lines and wrinkles on their faces. You know that they are looking for some hope that can keep the signs of aging at bay, even as they continue to get older. You happen to sell cosmetics and some of them are "age-defying" products. While you can't say that it removes wrinkles, since it's not true, you can give the hope and the illusion that it does.

It's not just the words you use to describe your products that can give this future promise of better things to come. In some cases, people have even relied on time lapse photography to prove that their products do produce a noticeable effect of smoothing out wrinkles with continued use. Other than getting a Botox injection, they may decide to spend some money and a little effort to see if your product works, completely on the basis of hope. One thing they do know, doing nothing will not produce any change in their lives. So, hope will spur them to buy when things are bad and doing nothing is worse than taking a risk to see if they can find some solution to their problems.

You are not going to hand out any guarantees that aren't true. There are plenty of ways to create a dream or a fantasy illusion of better things to come, by buying into the product. You can have people who used it give testimonials to convince other people that the product produced some change in their lives for the better. This can help bolster the claim the product is really a "miracle" product.

This strategy helps to create more sales, although it doesn't necessarily deliver everything that the dream or fantasy promises. That's because for some people it will work well and for others not. You can't determine really how many people will use your product the way it was intended or exactly what percentage of people will get good results. So, you can't make any guarantees or assure anyone that it is a 100% failsafe way of changing their situation. You do know, like them, that trying nothing is a sure way to fail though. So why not try something different?

And, that's why you have to remind people of the problem that bought them there. Maybe it was those wrinkles staring them in the face. In that case, you can talk about how devastating it is to see those lines accumulating with no end in sight. You can put up an image of a person with wrinkles and one without to show how different you would feel if you just managed to solve this one problem. So, in order to stimulate hope, you also have to remind people why they need change.

The psychological triggers

People can't live satisfying lives in a situation of despair. Suicides and addiction problems often manifest when people lack hope. So, hope truly is a positive emotion. It helps one to imagine things as they could be, and not as they are. This often spurs people to take action in situations that seem completely unresolvable. If they just focused on what was wrong with their lives and had no hope, they create a self-fulfilling prophecy that keeps them where they are at. While it's important to remind people why they need hope, they have to believe it is possible to do something to create change in their lives or they do not take action.

So, there are two psychological aspects you need to address when you are marketing using a trigger of hope. You have to remind people of how bad things are and you have to make the possibility of a new life possible. While the mind may be completely stumped as to how that's going to occur, you can still tap into other areas of the mind like intuition and feeling that are willing to believe in things it can't see. That's why it's important to have dreams in your life. Without dreams, we can't see our way out of our present predicaments.

Dreams and fantasies inspire us to be something that we currently are not. They give us the confidence to believe that change is possible. They can sometimes even inform us of the steps to make those changes. When we land in the world of dreams and fantasies, that's when the mind's burden of depressing details is overcome and the light of something almost spiritual takes its place. We believe.

How to implement effectively

So, your role as a marketing person is to sell a dream to inspire hope. It's as simple as that. Even if you're not running for president, you can use this strategy to help you sell products based on what they can do to change your customer's lives for the better. To do that, you have to be someone that people have faith in and find credible. You can't just be a homeless person off the street. That would hardly be inspiring. Your story and your image have to inspire confidence and trust, just as your rhetoric will inspire hope.

So, be careful of your own public image and the image your company is promoting too. If you are selling acne medication, it pays to be a dermatologist when using this strategy. If you're not, then get testimonials from dermatologists as well as people who use the product. Your dream of clear skin has to be believable by being promoted by authority figures and experts. So, if you're not one, pay someone to use them as a testimonial.

A great way to incur authority is to add all the alphabet suit of letters associated with your degree of learning next to your name. Even if you aren't a PhD you can still have quite a few certificates and degrees to add distinguished looking letters next to your name. Also, if your product or company has won any awards, this can also help to heighten the image that you are responsible and credible authorities in your field.

Once you have that image in place of being someone "in the know" then you can start to create the dream of a better world. Some areas of the marketplace lend themselves better to this strategy than others. That's because some problems are merely annoying whereas others can invoke despair or a stubborn unwillingness to change on their own, a perfect breeding ground for hope.

Areas that work well with this strategy is the health and beauty industries. People get sick and old. That's a fact of life. Sometimes these things can really depress people who search out a multitude of ways to stave off the effects of aging or to find something to at least make them more comfortable in their illnesses. Even preventative methods like vitamins and exercise programs can create a great deal of hope for people who want healthier lifestyles, but don't know how to achieve it themselves. Once they understand that something is possible, by seeing other people like them who succeeded, they will want to buy this solution to help them overcome their intractable problems too.

And, you can spur that hope by showing the results of those people who bought your products or programs and succeeded in changing their lives completely! Testimonials and interviews are excellent things that can be posted on your site. When you use video for these types of advertisements, people can really engage the same thinking process that the individual in the video went through to make the decision to purchase and ultimately change their lives. And, you can even address objections this way by having the person interviewed explain what they objected to in the offer and how it was negligible or wrong to view it that way (reframe it).

Now, here's the really nice thing about this strategy. There will always be a certain number of people who believe but simply don't have the confidence to take on a program of change on their own. They want to be led by the hand and they are willing to pay to do that from someone they respect or trust. This makes this strategy perfect for services such as coaching, counseling, and consultations. So, you can have a number of products that help people attempt the programs on their own, and then you can also have other services where people can sign up for private consultations or services that will help them to get over any obstacles as they arise.

And, that's not all

You would be able to train other people in the methods and programs that you are selling and create franchises or affiliates of people who are also experts in the system or product. They can pay you to teach them how to sell based on hope and change and they will go out to find new converts. The hope you sell to the affiliates is a hope of riches from mining the same rich vein of despair or problems that people are trying to resolve in mass. The hope you sell to the customers is the actual potential to resolve their problems. In this case, you can't sell an actual solution, just the dream or possibility of a solution, since it will depend on their ability to stick with a program and how it works on them in particular.

Timing this strategy

Keep an eye out for issues that will generate massive despair or anxiety in the public. Right now, home foreclosures and financial concerns are paramount in most people's mind. We hear of suicides and crime going up. This is the perfect time to sell a product that might help people in these markets. Of course, if they are having financial problems they may not have much cash, so you will have to figure out ways they can finance a purchase and still resolve their problem.

As the baby boomers age, you can expect the demand for products that keep them mobile, healthy, and active will increase. This massive demographic is prime for the selling on this strategy. In particular, this demographic has always wanted to do things in new and novel ways, so they are very receptive to change. All one has to do is time their product, service, or program to this growing market and the timing couldn't be more perfect for hope and change.

The timing in this strategy is based on market timing more than timing what you say or do. Of course, you want to know when to apply this strategy in the greater marketplace. For that you have to listen to the social issues going on and what problems are arising for a great number of people. You want to target the demographic with those problems. Then, you want to add websites and offers that appeal to those people based on hope and change. If you do it before you consider the market, this strategy will work, but it will have a greater impact if you time it to coincide with the greater issues going on at large in society.

CHAPTER 6

WHAT RICH MARKETERS HIDE FROM POOR MARKETERS

In this bonus section you will see some of the things that the rich marketers try to keep away from the poor marketers.

As you read these things, you will find out that there is not much that people do not know... The rich marketers try to reach new products earlier and try to dominate.

If you want to make the transition from being a poor marketer to being a rich marketer, then these are the points that you should read quite closely.

Many of those who today are well-known entrepreneurs, successful and mega rich have one thing in common with each other. Each of them was at one stage poor students or bankrupt business people who refused to give up.

They started with a dream, an idea that began as a spark and that spark of an idea grew into the multimillion-dollar companies with which their names are synonymous. What created the success for them? What was the key to their success when so many others have failed?

1. They had a dream and they lived that dream and did not give up on that dream. That dream was a

big dream and it drove them. They believed their dream even when failure looked them in the face.

2. They learned from mistakes and turned mistakes into success. They used failure as a learning tool to enable them to consider how to do things better next time.

3. They started small and gradually built up. Their focus was on building a niche and being the best in that niche. They did not allow their focus to become too big too quickly. This is the sure recipe for success.

4. Their focus was not on the income but on the product and building a loyal base of supporters through the product (or service) they were offering. Networking was the key, it produced the market, and it produced the opportunity for expansion. They did not need to do it alone. Others bought into their dream.

5. They explored and utilized every available marketing strategy to build their dreams, with the focus firmly on building social networks to develop strong customer focused and customer driven products and services. Therefore, the products sold themselves.

6. They invested time and energy into the development of businesses that eventually produced income with little or no effort on their part.

7. They explored and understood social and economic trends to ensure they understood where the market was going and historically what to expect, understanding that history often repeats itself.

8. They focused their time, energy, and resources on the outcomes of their research, and invested accordingly, rather than following the crowd.

9. Although at times they did hesitate, they kept the dream and did not allow setbacks to destroy the dream, but having learned from the setback, they allowed themselves to continue the dream and take risks.

10. As they took risks, they did not lose sight of their objective to create successful businesses and have an income source that did not rely totally on their involvement to be successful.

Those who have failed in business are those who have allowed the current economic climate drive their business decisions they have failed to do their research. They do not understand the rise and fall of the markets and the wealth cycles. This has prevented them from taking full advantage of investments and portfolios that create income and lose what income they have earned. They have accumulated debt rather than focusing on escaping the debt cycle and failed to see the money market for what it is.

They have succumbed to their failures and been scared off by them and they have given into the market trend that suggests that you cannot make money in today's economic climate as a business person.

Robert Kiyosaki has the last word:

"The size of your success is measured by the strength of your desire, the size of your dream and how you handle disappointment along the way."

CHAPTER 7

BIG WEALTH AND
THE LAW OF ATTRACTION

With the release of The Secret followed by the outstanding response it has garnered, a lot of people are speaking about the Law of Attraction. The problem is that not half of these people know what they are talking about.

The Law of Attraction is not an enchantment or a potion that will wish all your problems away. There are things that need to be done if you want to experience its richness in your life.

This chapter specifically deals with the implementation of the Law of Attraction in gathering money, but really it is about all its various applications that can help in improving your life.

Sit back, free up your mind from all its clutter, and have a good read.

The Law of Attraction –
What it really is and what it is not

Let us begin by understanding what the Law of Attraction really is all about.

It is somewhat amazing to see how much talk there is about the Law of Attraction and how few people actually know about what it is. The Law of Attraction is not a spell that you use and things begin happening that way. It is not that you chant, like begets a thousand times a day and see things happening the way you want. If the Law of Attraction were so simple, we would have already witnessed the world as a much better place by now.

People explain the Law of Attraction in various ways. The common definition you will find will be something like this:

"If you strongly believe that something should happen, it will certainly happen."

A sentence couldn't be any simpler, but you will immediately realize that this raises more questions than it answers. The question of desires is the most important. Is it only what we desire and think about strongly that will happen? Or will things that we don't desire also happen if we somehow think strongly about them? Then there is also the question of internal conflict of thoughts. At times, there could be situations where we think equally in both ways. For example, we may think that a job could be ours or not. So how do we apply the Law of Attraction in such a case? Or what do we do when we are thinking strongly about something and someone else is thinking strongly about the exact opposite thing? What will happen in that case?

In order to be able to reply to all these questions, it is important to first understand what the Law of Attraction really says.

Notwithstanding the various ways in which the Law of Attraction has been defined, we can break things down in the following four elements:

- We must know exactly what we want.

- We must begin a thought process for it, and begin vociferously asking the universe to make it happen.

- We must then visualize a situation wherein we already have what we are hankering for, and we must live in that reality.

- At the same time, we must not attach ourselves to what might happen. We must only think about having it. There is no room for apprehension.

In this chapter, we are going to expose various aspects of the Law of Attraction and see how we can apply it in one of the most important areas of our lives – attracting money. Can one really become rich by just thinking vividly about it? We need to understand the law better and learn how to implement it in order to get these answers.

Objective and subjective thinking

Since the Law of Attraction is so strongly based in the thought process, we must first learn what our thought processes really are.

One of the main steps toward understanding the Law of Attraction to a greater degree is to understand what the word "thought" really means. Throughout the description of this law, you will find that it doesn't refer to thinking in the way that we do. We think that we exist, we are in a particular situation, there are certain people with and around us, there are things we are with and so on. Whatever we see becomes real for us, and that becomes a part of our thought. However, this is not the kind of thought process that the Law of Attraction talks about. This is known as objective thinking.

But, in order to see the implementation of the Law of Attraction in our lives, we have to first shun the concept of objective thinking. We have to adopt a higher level of thinking, which is subjective thinking.

Why do we think that our spouse is real? Because we can see them. But this is objective thinking.

With subjective thinking, things will be the other way round. We think our spouse is real and therefore we see them. Now, that is subjective thinking.

Your job isn't real. But because you believe so concretely that it is real, it becomes a reality for you.

Your situations aren't real. However, your firm belief that they are happening makes them real for you.

This is the realm of subjective thinking. When you think subjectively, things are more or less like how you are seeing a dream. When we see a dream, how do we picture ourselves? Is our "dream" self the real us? No, we are the ones who are "seeing" the dream. We are just the frame of reference, the consciousness.

Whatever is happening in our dream is our perspective. That is how thinking works in the subjective world.

In this world, what we see is actually just a manifestation of our thoughts. Now, that doesn't mean those things aren't real. What that means is that those things are present in our consciousness. Just as we might be able to alter things in our dreams, by applying the Law of Attraction, we could alter things in our "real" life as well.

Stop the default processes from ruling your life

We give a lot of focus to things that are irrelevant in our lives, so much so that they actually start ruling our existence. But there are ways in which we can stop them from toying with us.

To a large extent, we allow things and situations to rule over us. How many times in life do we tell, "This situation is beyond me"! "I cannot do anything about it." We do that a lot. Each time that we do that, we are yielding the control of our lives to the situations that are governing us. We do not think even one bit in the way that the Law of Attraction suggests us to do.

And what is that way?

Quite simply put, that way is to think as though we rule the circumstances. The fact is that these circumstances are much in our hands. It is up to us to create situations that are conducive for our development, and not the other way round.

Think about it. Is a financial problem bogging you down? You have probably planned an endeavor but aren't able to do so because of paucity of funds. So what do you do? Most people will think that this is going nowhere and they will bail themselves out. But a person who really believes subjectively will understand that the financial problem lies in the frame of reference and will not worry about it too much. On the other hand, such a person will try to think that he or she could make the situation conducive.

Sounds impractical? It isn't so impractical actually. If you begin to think strongly about having money, what will you do? The Law of Attraction tells you that you have to "visualize" it and actually behave as though you have the money. In that case, you will apply for a loan probably and when you do that, you will be very confident because you believe that the money will be yours. Your confidence will work to your advantage because your potential financiers will get the impression that you have the capability to earn and pay them back. They understand you are a person of merit.

This is what the believers in the Law of Attraction do. They make things conducive to them through an intense thought process. But their thought process is not of this objective world. They think as though they are the center of everything that's happening and that they can have full control over the situations they face.

Pivoting your thought process

So how do you go about developing this kind of thought process, where you think you are the center of the universe and everything just exists in your frame of reference?

In order to create the subjective thought process that the Law of Attraction demands of you, it is very important that you create the right frame of reference. You have to be like the person seeing everything in a dream. Your perceived reality is actually the things that are happening in your frame of reference, which is just another name for your consciousness. But, you need to put a finger on this consciousness. You need to anchor it. This aspect – anchoring your conscious mind – is known as pivoting your thought process.

When you begin pivoting your thought process, the primary requirement is to have a fixed point from where you can begin. Usually, this fixed point is your resolve, your intention, your motive, your purpose. For example, if you really need to start a business, your resolution to do that is your pivot. The stronger you resolve to achieve that, the more profound your pivot will be. That is why people who have stronger resolutions are able to achieve better things than people who don't have a very strong mindset to achieve something.

If you consider your desire as your pivot and see everything from that perspective, everything begins falling into place.

You feel as though everything that's happening is happening as a means of bringing you closer to your desire. In the above instance, if your desire to start a business is your pivot, then you feel as though everything happening in your life is taking you one step closer toward realizing your dreams. This includes the positives as well as negatives. If you suddenly meet someone, you feel that somehow that will be connected with your new business, which isn't yet started but you have no apprehensions in your mind about it. You also feel that you're getting fired from your desk job was something that will take you closer to having your own business.

People who believe in the Law of Attraction staunchly build such pivots in their minds. From then on, their entire life is focused on this pivot. This is what drives them and motivates them into coming closer to their goals.

The right mindset about money

We are applying the Law of Attraction to wealth. What is important here is the mindset that we need to make this application.

What does the Law of Attraction tell us about money?

It is actually very important to point out that the Law of Attraction is not just about money. It is a very general law which can be applied to every aspect of our lives. This is a law that helps to enrich ourselves as people, not just financial entities. However, we are endeavoring to see how we can apply the Law of Attraction as regards to attracting money.

That is the reason it becomes vital to know what kind of mindset you must have. If we try to implement the Law of Attraction to this concept, we must realize that a person who is actually trying to attract money should think about it all the time. Since thoughts attract results, this is what must happen.

However, the thoughts mustn't be objective. What are objective thoughts? Now, if you are only thinking about how many dollars you will earn on a particular project, then that is objective thinking. If you cannot think beyond numbers, all you are doing is thinking objectively. You are thinking how much you could make, how much you could save, etc. These are objective thoughts and, if you were to apply the Law of Attraction, you would understand that these thoughts won't attract the money to you.

Hence, you need to think subjectively. Don't think about the money itself, but think about what you must do in order to bring the money to you. Thinking about the quality of your product, for example, is a beautiful step in this regard. When you do that, you are actually improving the sales potential of your product and hence you are bringing in the money.

A person who believes in the Law of Attraction won't think – "I must sell this product because I want to earn money." Instead, such a person would think – "I must be honest in making this product and give it great quality so that I earn money out of it."

A person believing in the Law of Attraction automatically becomes honest because he or she knows what it takes to bring in the money. They don't believe in quick-fix solutions but always go for the long haul. This should be your mindset about money too – Don't think about how to actually bring in the money; think about what you must do in order to let the money come to you.

Wealth manifestation through the Law of Attraction

The five steps you need in order to manifest wealth applying the Law.

Wealth Manifestation through the Law of Attraction. Here are the five things you need to do in order to manifest the wealth that you are expecting through the Law of Attraction.

Believe

The first step is to ingrain the thought of wealth in your subconscious. You have to think staunchly that you will be able to attain the large amount of wealth that you are hoping for.

Visualize

It is very important to actually visualize the wealth. You have to think that the wealth is already in your bank account and now what you will do with it. Begin thinking as if you are planning what to do with the money. You don't have it already, but that's not the point. The Law of Attraction tells that you have to be strong in your belief, and visualization is the best way to do that.

Be grateful

Taking your belief one step forward, you must actually start thanking the universe for granting the wealth to you. Well, it has not already granted you the wealth, but you have no aspersions at all about that happening. You are darned sure that you will get the wealth and so being grateful is the next logical thing.

Listen to your heart

Your heart will tell you a lot of things at this point. It will tell you to do particular things. Do not stifle any of these "voices". Listen to them intently. Act upon them.

You have to make sure that you listen to every voice because any of them could be the one voice that opens the doors of opportunity to you.

Continue your actions

Never give up, never relent. Remember that stopping is a sign of weakness. You don't want the universe to understand that your belief is faltering. You want it to know that you will keep up no matter what. Sooner or later, your supreme confidence is going to bring the wealth at your door.

Is a poor person who thinks positively about money rich?

Does only thought matter? If beggars think about horses, can they ride?

This is a question that irks most people, especially those who hear about the Law of Attraction for the first time. After all, they think, the Law of Attraction speaks about thoughts begetting results, so if they were to think strongly about something, shouldn't they get that realized? In other words, if someone doesn't have a car and thinks strongly about it, they should be owners of the car, right?

Though that does sound very romantic, the problem is that the Law of Attraction does not work in that fashion. It is not about think- think-get-get. There are a lot of under layers here. Firstly, people who think about the Law of Attraction in this manner don't bring a very important thing into the equation – the emphasis of effort. You don't get much without channelizing your thoughts into action.

Let us understand this better with an example. Suppose you have an ambition to open a restaurant. Right now, it's just your ambition.

Yes, you are thinking so strongly about it that you can taste it, but that's just about it. Will that make your restaurant then?

The answer is quite obvious – No. The Law of Attraction is not about sitting on your bean bag watching a DVD and expecting your inner desires to manifest themselves. You have to actually let the thought out of your system. You have to let it come out and become action.

When you think strongly about something, there will be an inner voice that will tell you to act in a particular way. If you are looking at opening a restaurant, a small voice within you will tell you to start hunting for good places. The voice will tell you to learn the art of hotel management. The voice will also tell you to begin gathering funds. There are so many things that will be spoken by this still small voice. The important thing is that you have to listen to it. And you have to act upon it.

It is only when you begin translating these thoughts into actions will you be able to do something about realizing them.

So a beggar who merely thinks about a horse won't be able to do something soon. However, if he thinks how he should get the horse and start implementing those ideas, there is all likelihood that he will be atop one soon enough.

What about lotteries and windfall incomes?

What does the Law of Attraction have to say about lotteries and all other kinds of overnight richness modes?

A very commonly asked question by most people is whether they can win lotteries and have other kinds of lucky breaks merely by having a strong belief in them, just as the Law of Attraction would have them do. They think very strongly about winning and so why should they not win? They even think about winning all the time, they buy tickets by the dozen, so the winners should be them, right?

The problem is that these people are in the right premise, but they aren't implementing it in the right way. So, what's the right way? Can you use the Law of Attraction to win a lottery?

Well, for that, the first thing is to think rightly about it. You must not expect a spell to come into action bringing gold coins at your door. This won't happen. But you could align things to work your way. Think positively about winning. When you do that, things automatically begin happening in a way that's beneficial to you. You probably won't become a millionaire overnight, but maybe your strong beliefs will help you win small amounts and be happy about them.

But there are ways in which you can go against the Law of Attraction here. If you expect too much, it's wrong. The Law of Attraction tells you to have a strong belief, but it does not tell you to expect a particular kind of result. Simply visualize what would happen if you are a winner of a particular sum, however, don't force the universe into granting you that sum. In the same vein, if you start getting grumpy if you are not making the kind of income you think you should, you are undoing all your positive belief. Grumpiness is a sign of disbelief and hence it is a sign of weakness.

People who win lotteries think somehow that they deserved the victory. If you were to ask them, they will say that they visualized winning the lottery at some point in their lives and they imagined it so vividly that they felt it was for real.

Try that. Imagine. Visualize your result. Don't go over-board. Don't over-expect. Things will begin aligning your way. But be ready to accept, without grudging, whatever comes your way. It will be better than what you have, if your belief is in the right.

Balancing the inner self and the outer self

If you really follow the Law of Attraction, you have to work at striking the right balance between your inner and outer selves.

One of the most significant applications of the Law of Attraction is to balance our inner and outer selves. Our inner self is our consciousness. It is the way we think and behave. This is where the Law of Attraction begins to take effect. The Law of Attraction starts manifesting itself when we think and that begins in our inner self. Our outer self is characterized by our action. The way we act and implement our thought processes is how our outer self-functions.

If we have to make the best utilization of the Law of Attraction into our life, then it is essential that we learn how to create the balance between our inner and outer selves. It is vital that we put into action what we think. What begins as a thought manifestation must get converted into action.

If you were to just think and sit about getting a new house, it isn't going to happen. Yes, if your thoughts are strong, if your belief is strong, the universe will begin aligning itself toward making things happen. But now, it is you who has to act. If you don't even lift a finger things aren't going to happen. Now, you have to put your outer self into action. This is when the positive energies that have been created start taking shape and things begin happening.

The problem with most of us is that we use our inner self to think and believe. We say so often that we want to do a particular thing but only a few of us actually put our outer selves into action mode.

The Law of Attraction will make things happen. But it will restrict itself to aligning things in a particular way. The rest is your call. It will make you confident about doing certain things, and that is what will influence the people around you and things will happen positively for you, but the main thing for that to happen is that you have to take the initiative and act.

Why doesn't everyone that uses the law of attraction become rich?

A lot of people might think about the Law of Attraction. But only a few of them actually begin climbing the steps of success and really become rich.

If you have been following through so far, you will have realized two things:

- The Law of Attraction is a definite reality; everyone puts it to use.
- However, a lot of people don't really put it to use the right way.

There is no refuting the strength of the Law of Attraction in channelizing the energies of the universe in such a way that things can begin to happen favorably. But the problem is that, the Law of Attraction will only channelize these things. If we don't make use of the energies to achieve what we are hankering after, it's all going to be a lost cause.

For example, if you only think about becoming rich but don't do anything actively in that regard, there's no way that you will become rich. In fact, even if you win through a lottery, you have to make the effort of buying the lottery and tracking the winnings.

The bottom line is clear – the Law of Attraction works but only if you put it to use. These are the things that you must do sequentially:

- You must strongly believe that a particular thing will happen. Your belief should be strong and unwavering, so unshakable that nothing must twist your belief in any way.
- Then you have to visualize this thing, as though it has actually happened with you and that you are enjoying its fruits.
- The next step will be to begin acting upon your inner voice. You will hear your inner voice a lot when you strongly believe in something. Acting upon this is what will bring you closer to realizing your ambitions.

So, if you are planning on becoming rich through the Law of Attraction, the important thing for you is to believe and then act. Without either of them, nothing is going to fall into place.

Conclusion

The Law of Attraction can make you rich. You must have heard it a lot. Now you know what it takes to get there.

CHAPTER 8

EXPLOIT BUSINESS OPPORTUNITIES LIKE THE WEALTHY

The person who can understand and act upon opportunities is the one that succeeds in life. We speak too much about being there at the right time and the right place, but what does this really mean? What happens to those who aren't there at the right time and the right place? Don't they get their opportunities?

In this chapter we will show you how to understand business opportunities and make the most of them in your life.

Business Opportunities – What are the qualities of a great business opportunity?

How do you make sure that the business opportunity staring at you is good for you? Here are some points.

The first step of any successful business is to find out about the quality of the business opportunity you are planning to start. You should know what you must look for.

The following are a few qualities that you need to check before you start any business. There are more, of course, but these are the ones that you should absolutely not miss out on:

1. The business should have enough targeted customer base. Now, what do we mean by that? Let's say you are planning to start a home-based business. You will need to look for a business that is more in demand. Where need is high and supply is less, you can have a better scope of success. Take the example of SEO opportunities for freelancers. You can do this from home without any high investment. In this niche, the requirement on your part is very high and you are bound to do well if you put in the right effort, because the professionals here are fewer. You need such an opportunity.

2. The business should have a good breakeven point. If your business doesn't have that, then you need to have large amount of working capital. Making a project report that tells how much you will have to put in and how much you will get from the business, and when, is a great idea.

3. Your interest in the business you start is highly important. There are many people who start a business looking at its potential, but don't reach the level they desire, primarily because they don't have much interest in the business itself.

4. Before starting with the business opportunity, see to it that you get proper resources on time, like manpower, guidance, consulting, financial credit if needed, infrastructure, etc.

5. Check before only if your business is over competitive or over in demand, if competitiveness is very high it will be difficult for you to get established in the business soon.

So, in summary, you need to check out all the pluses and minuses of the business opportunity before you plan to start anything. Once you start, it can get very difficult to stop. Being forewarned is being better-armed.

Where to look for business opportunities?

Opportunities don't usually happen; usually you have to look for them.

Now, as you know what to looking for in a business opportunity, you should also know where to find them, get new ideas and more. So just keep on reading – here are some "Best Practice" strategies on how to find best business opportunities.

Method 1 - Search Engines – Your Gold Mine of Information

Search engines are the best place to find the information for any business. You can say search engines are gold mines of information. You could just do a common search on Google or Yahoo! and find out about thousands of business opportunities. But, of course, you wouldn't know which of these are good to have and which aren't, in which case, you might have to read their reviews as well, which again you will find through search engines. Look for specific forums on business opportunities where you will find people talking about them and giving their opinions.

Method 2 – Join Business Forums (Online as well as Offline)

Forums are now a day's very much in demand especially online. There are many business forums having around 2 to 3 million users. Using forums you can discuss get professional help, advice from experts and also from people who are searching for business opportunities. Just Google the keyword of your business with the word "forums" and you will get a list of top forums in that niche.

Method 3 – Classified Ads (Don't Ignore These)

Regularly check newspapers, TV news, online news, online press release where on a daily bases thousands of business opportunities are posted. Just take advantage of this revolution and get great ideas for the best business opportunities.

Method 4 – Get Memberships into Top Clubs

Clubs are one of the best places where people go for entertainment and also share their business experience and resources. Here you can get lots and lots of business ideas and great opportunities. Be social in top clubs and see how you can grow your business with new business opportunities.

Method 5 – Get Information from Government Bodies

Governments do provide many good business opportunities in terms of grants, information help, leads and many other resources. This source is one of the most trusted sources. Get in touch with your local business regulation bodies to get a long list of business information and ideas.

Successful people aren't born successful; they understand and accept new opportunities

People aren't born with success written all over them. You might be born in a rich household, but that's not a guarantee that you will be rich individually as well. Here's what successful people do – they keep their ear open for any news of new opportunities.

No one is born successful. When we are born we don't even know how to spell successful, knowing its meaning is something quite far- off. When we grow up, we begin chipping away at it in the efforts to turn our lives into successful lives. Some of us do achieve the success that we have thought about, but that doesn't come without a great deal of effort.

One of the most important ingredients in becoming successful is to have a vision, a dream. If you don't know how to dream, you will most probably not achieve anything in life. Some people are afraid to dream, thinking they would be terribly frustrated if they don't achieve their goals. But the fact is that if you don't dream, you probably won't get it. Great people dreamed of flying, going to moon and so on... you see now that we can fly, we can go to moon.

In this age when people are thinking how to build gadgets that can turn objects and even people invisible, it is quite unwise to restrict one's thoughts. What do you dream about? You may dream about having a great business or buying a home or a car of your own. In the light of all the achievements that people have made, do you think all this is as difficult as you think? This shows there is nothing impossible in this world if you do it the right way, if you take initiative and plan it properly.

Just take the example of Bill Gates, my favorite example actually. Practically the whole world today uses his Microsoft products, not realizing that these products belong to a person who was a computer class dropout. Take a look at Facebook. It started as a college project and has today made a revolution in the field of social networking. How can we not talk about Google, which started in a dingy office and today it dominates our online world.

All these successes have been achieved in just a few short years! So what's your excuse?

Don't lose hope, hold on to your big dreams and try to achieve them. The simple steps that you need to take are hard work, and to hit the right time and the right place. Follow this and no one can stop you from reaching your goals. Plan things properly on paper before executing them. Make milestones for yourself and give yourself rewards once you reach them.

Why we should always be on the move!

Success rarely comes to people who wait in the wings for things to happen to them. It happens to people who stay on the move.

I have seen thousands of people fail in their lives due to only one reason, i.e. they don't take action. Let's say you have $10 million but you don't know how and where to use those millions. The amount becomes worthless to you then. So, if you have resources, information and a business plan, make it a point to execute them. Don't just keep them on paper.

Some people work very hard during the initial stages of their business, but if they don't succeed early on, they stop. You must know that success most probably won't come instantly. You need be dedicated and sometimes work for years to get real success. But some people get demotivated very quickly. Most of these people have not planned for the worst and they don't have back up plans. Keep all these things ready and keep working on your plans and you will see that you will move closer to success.

Failure is not the only reason why people stop working. In some people, overconfidence becomes the primary culprit. These are the people who succeed early on, but then they become overconfident about their achievements, which even makes them complacent.

They start thinking they have achieved everything and now they don't need to do much, but the fact is we should never stop and should always be on the move to achieve more and more success.

Then, there are other kinds of people who just keep dreaming, keep thinking they will do one thing or the other, but the fact is they just need to execute those plans. Everyone can dream but only those people who work hard can achieve those dreams.

Identifying great business opportunities and acting upon them!

It isn't enough to just listen to your opportunity's call. You have to act upon it.

There should be a formula to make a great successful business and plan to take action on that formula which should be executed properly by acting upon them.

There are a few things you need to take care of which will help you to take action on your plan.

- Always expect and shoot for the best
- Create your work plan on paper

- Dedicate yourself to work and complete the tasks on time
- Make milestones for your plan
- Make schedules for daily, weekly and monthly task and don't miss them
- Always keep a backup plan which keeps you in the business

Sometimes we work very hard but at the end of the day we are not satisfied with our work. This usually results in poor outcomes. This happens if you work without a plan. So always make a complete plan on paper.

Give yourself targets and gifts too. We always need some kind of motivation to keep our self in business with good standing. Let's say you had to complete a task by tomorrow evening but you complete it in the morning, then give yourself some reward. This rises your opinion of yourself, which is very important.

Plan your tasks with backup plans, say you are not able to complete the task on time for some reason. Ensure that you have something else prepared to cover that time. Fill it in with another task!

Always prioritize your tasks. Sequence them in the order of their importance. There should be a "must-do task" for daily or weekly basis. This gives you a chance to complete your important work at least in a week and don't miss it.

If you don't know how to make a plan, get help from professionals such as accountants and other financial experts, but don't start without a plan. 90% of businesses fail because they don't have a plan on paper. At the same time, implementing the plan is of supreme importance as well.

Does opportunity knock twice?

There is a saying that failure is the first step toward success. Many people stop their efforts when they have failed once. They fall prey to thinking that if they have failed once, they won't be able to do well again. However, opportunities do recur in life; you just have to be ready and grab them when they come again. You should not opt out of accepting these opportunities when they come by you again.

Nine out of ten people who are successful today have faced failure sometime in their lives. Francis Ford Coppola was a washout when his important directorial venture was proclaimed a dud when it was being filmed. However, he continued his efforts unrelenting, and that "dud" is known today as the classic The Godfather. A person of average mindset would have given up when people began to become critical, but he didn't and he gave us one of our greatest cinematic masterpieces of all time.

This is simply a learning process. When we started school in our childhood, we didn't know a lot of things. We learned everything by committing mistakes and fixing them. That's the part that contributes to our success. If you've faced failure before, you will be more successful as you know what to do if you face that kind of conditions in the future.

So it does not matter if we lost the opportunity once or twice, it keeps coming. Let me give you a live example. You were waiting for a bus to go somewhere, and for some reason, you missed one bus, what do you do? Don't you try for another bus to reach your destination or do you return to where you were before? Just as you wait for the bus and catch it the next time it arrives, you wait for opportunities as well. And, just like buses do, opportunities come by you again as well.

If your efforts are correct and meaningful, there is no reason why you should not succeed in them. Opportunities knock several times in life, but you have to be ready to accept them in the right way, and surely you will be able to tackle them as you have learned many things from your past failures.

So never get too depressed, keep trying your best and one day you will be scaling new heights of success.

Using the internet to "discover" your business opportunities

The Internet is one of the best places to discover business opportunities; there are many options available here where you can do research, gather data, research papers and so on. We are going to speak about some of the best methods to find what is more in demand and what people are looking for.

1. You can do research on practically any product or service using search engines. You can find how many competitors there are, what they are promoting, how long they have been in business, what their USP is, at what price they sell at and so on. You can easily get all the needed information from search engines. Simply enter you keyword and you get all the information you need.

2. You can try Google Trends (http://www.google.com/trends), this tool helps you to see what's currently in demand. For an example, you can find out what the trends are from the past or up to the minute today! This tool will let you know how in demand a product is or was in the past.

3. You can try http://pulse.ebay.com, http://www.amazon.com and magazine websites. These websites give you details of which product or business section is more in demand, which product users are searching for, what people are buying and so on. If you go to magazine websites you can find out which products are highlighted as those websites will only display products or service which are in current demand, so we can use their ideas.

4. You can use the Google External Keyword Tool (https://adwords.google.com/select/KeywordToolExternal) which give you total search volume of a particular keyword which people are searching, for example keyword "weight loss" was searched 20,400,000 times in just one month by American users.

So, you see there are many ways to get information on different business opportunities. Just explore it.

Listening to an opportunity is not enough; you have to put it into action.

What you must do when an opportunity comes your way. When you work for someone it makes it easier for you, typically they take all the risk, guide you, and inform you what to do and how to do it. But when you choose to start your own business it's a totally new game. The main part to starting your own business, be it your entrepreneur business or home based, you need to take action, action and action.

You should not only plan on what to do, when to do and how to do, but also implement the plan you have made. As it's your business you only have to take action, no one else will do that for you.

One of the most important reasons for people not achieving success is lack of hard work, or commitment to themselves. You need to execute your plan instantly. Merely thinking about the opportunity at the drop of a hat and trying to implement it isn't going to take you anywhere.

If you work hard and execute your plans as per plan, you will surely get the rewards which you expected and many times much more than expected.

There is a saying that action speaks louder than words. So put your plans into action and see how it gives you returns. You don't get anything just by speaking it out; you need to actually do that. It's not difficult to be a go getter or put your plans into action. Just be confident, be committed to yourself and you will see the results. There is unlimited potential for hardworking people and for those who put their plans in action and not just listen to an opportunity to become successful.

Inspiring people to help you reach your goals

It will be very difficult to plow on without the support of people whom you can trust. The best people are those whom you can inspire. Reaching your goal is not as difficult as many think. You can reach your goal if you follow some of the common techniques from real life. Let me show you one very simple example of a "word of mouth" marketing technique. Let's say you have to buy a T.V, what do you do? Ask your friends what TV is the best? Get reviews online? Get expert advice? Right? Yes, we do all this before buying or taking action. This is really a very simple marketing technique of involving more and more people to help you promote your business. If they like the product or service they will surly promote it to others without any charge as they want to give the best to their friends and family.

Take an example of MLM it's totally based on "word of mouth" marketing. One person joins the network and he invites others to join and then others invite more people and so on. This way, the company reaches its target easily without much marketing and concentrating on quality of the product.

You too can follow the same method, join more and more clubs, more and more events and spread your network. The more networks of people you have, the more easily you can reach your goals. Indirectly you help them and they help you. It's a kind of a win-win situation. You make a friend, which is fun and it helps you to reach your goal.

Can anything be better than this?

So start joining clubs, groups, events, parties, tours and make friends and groups and reach your goals easily without any errors.

Don't stop with just one opportunity

The most successful individuals in the world have been unstoppable. I can say that 99% of people are not satisfied with what they have. Like a person who has a motorcycle will want a car, those who have a car want a luxury car, those who have a luxury car want to have a private jet and so on. This is the nature of humans and that's why we are successful as we always have dreams that keep life moving forward in a positive light.

So when we have so many dreams do you think success can be achieved with just one successful opportunity or business? When we want everything why don't we try to grab more and more opportunities which give us everything we need in life?

The fact is most of the world's richest people have multiple stream of income from multiple businesses. They started with one business and now have multiple ventures to their names. We think that we invested xyz amount and we got good returns, so now everything is fine; but the fact is we always need more and for that we need to have more and more business opportunities.

Burger King started with a single restaurant, now it has franchisees all over the world. This is the power of looking for more opportunities to grow. If you stop at any point you are not going to fulfill the dreams of becoming rich and famous. Diversification is a very important aspect of getting at where you want to reach.

Conclusion

Opportunities come everyone's way but not a lot of people can understand what they should do with them. Most people don't even know where to look for the right opportunities.

But now you have a start. And the right motivation. Go forth and conquer.

CHAPTER 9

FINANCIAL EMPOWERMENT - EARNING THE GREENBACKS

Financial Empowerment is the buzzword for the new generation. This is the jet-set generation that wants to be self-sufficient in what they have, never have a need for more and keep attracting more even as they sleep.

But what makes them different from others who aren't financially empowered already? What can the have-nots of this generation do to elevate themselves to the status of the haves?

Most importantly, is this upward transition possible?

Here's what it takes in today's world to reach the top economic pedestals of society. This is what it takes to reach the Fortune 500 lists and then stay there.

What is financial empowerment?

Here's a look into what financial empowerment really means. The term "financial empowerment" has many aspects. On a general note, it means being self-sufficient with money, so much so that you don't keep wanting for more. You have your financial coffers full and for any of your needs, you just have to plunge into them and get at the money. A person who is financially empowered is thus dynamic economically as well because he or she is able to use money to attract more money.

This speaks about financial empowerment on an individual note. However, there is also a social aspect to it. Analysts also speak about financially empowering a particular section of people, such as empowering the youth or the seniors or the sick or the women. In each context, it means self-reliance. These particular sections of society are usually dependent on other active and earning classes for their monetary requirements. When economists speak about financially empowering these groups, what they mean is that these groups should be self- sufficient and not have to depend on others.

However, in this chapter we are going to confine ourselves to individual financial empowerment. We are going to speak about how an individual – that is you – can become self-reliant with money. It is a truly great feeling not having to depend on anyone else for your financial requirements and not everyone can do that. But if the right steps are taken, this is very much achievable.

The solutions mentioned in this chapter are going to be simple, but it is in the implementation of them that their true worth comes out. This is what you have to know. No financial empowerment techniques are of any value unless and until they are really implemented in the right away. The approaches must see action.

From here, we begin our journey to financial empowerment. Understand the concepts and implement them and you will see how they start working for you.

Ability v/s Action

Being able is one thing. That creates potential in you, but it doesn't empower you. The empowerment comes through putting your ability into action. There is a wide gulf between ability and action in the world that we live in. There are millions of people out there who are capable of doing something. They might even have the right academic qualifications and some might even have the experience. But then these people aren't putting their talents to the right use. Think about something that can teach excellently, but doesn't put that talent to use. This teacher is instead doing a desk job because according to him or her that's a safer bet. Now, the desk job can only take the person so far because he or she doesn't really like doing that stuff. However, if this person had taken the bigger step of going ahead and teaching – overcoming any limitations in the way, such as stage fright – it is highly possible that he or she would be much better financially stable and empowered today.

We all have various talents, but we fail to discover them and even if we do, we fail to put them to use. J. K. Rowling would not have become the multimillionaire she is today if she had given up her penchant for writing and chased a humdrum "safe" job like most of us do. Imagine Michael Schumacher or Zinedine Zidane's vast bundle of talent hidden behind an office job. Think what Barack Obama would have been if he did not act to implement his immense leadership potential and charisma to rule one of the most developed nations of the world.

The one thing we have to consider is that it is not just enough to be able. It is not enough to be able to swim, cook, dance, write, and jump or whatever. If you want to be financially empowered, you have to use these abilities that are within you and wow the people around you. It is only then that you start taking steps toward your empowerment.

The four fundamentals

If you are looking at financially empowering yourself, you cannot neglect these four important fundamentals. These are the ingredients you need to prepare this recipe of economic freedom. When you are looking at building yourself financially, there are a few things that you must make sure you have with you. These are your allies in your quest for financial empowerment – they are your four fundamentals – without which you will find this journey very difficult. Here we take a look at these four essentials in this chapter, we shall take a detailed look at what they really mean.

Assets

Assets are the material and nonmaterial things that you have with you. These things are valuable because you use them to create more things. However, we are going to bring about a change in your perspective of assets. Normally people think only about monetary assets. But everything that you have, including the love of your spouse, can become an asset.

Education

Education has veritable factors in empowering yourself financially because your career is going to depend on how educated you are. However, education does not just mean academic qualifications – everything that you do in the pursuit of achieving something counts toward your education. Even reading a manual to understand how a particular software application operates will be education for you because you can use it in the future in some other way to enrich what you have got.

Investment

Investing is an asset because this helps you in securing money for the long run. When things are going the way they shouldn't, your investments matter a lot. Even when everything is hunky-dory, your investments build up your financial portfolio like few other things can.

Recreation

You might not willingly take this as a factor for financial empowerment, but the fact is that you need to enrich your mind in order to stay healthier and hence make yourself more stable monetarily. Some forms of recreation can actually directly help in improving your economic standing as well.

The Sum of Five

The Sum of Five is the essential law that helps you to evolve financially so that you keep moving upward. The Sum of Five is a key aspect in financial empowerment. It is a rule, a rule which you apply in order to keep yourself dynamic. It ensures that you don't remain stuck in the rut when you have achieved a modicum of success, but you keep improving upon it and keep moving northward.

So, what does the Sum of Five state?

The Sum of Five states that if your income is the sum total of the five people closest to you. If the five most prominent people you are dealing with financially make less money than you do, then it is time for you to find some more financial collaborators.

This is the statement of the Sum of Five, but you need not judge it by what it actually says. Look at what it means. What it means is this – When you are involved in a business collaboration with several people, you must take a look at how much the five people closest to you are earning. Here, we don't really mean a number at all. The "five" is irrelevant. You have to look at the people you are dealing with at all times. If the people you are dealing with are making more money than you are, you must continue your efforts till you reach their level. But if they are all making less money than you, it means you have reached a point of stagnancy and now you need to find more people to hobnob with.

You won't be mistaken if you find this law to be a bit selfish. Actually, it isn't that way. We all believe and accept that change is imminent. We say that all the time. Then why do we not change the circumstances that surround us? We tend to live in the same situation for life, without trying to think we should take higher leaps. This is where we make the absolute error.

If we want to progress, it is important for us to improve the situation that we are surrounded with. It is important for us to change the set of people we regularly deal with. There is a saying in an Indian language that says, "A man doesn't really succeed in life unless he leaves his childhood behind." What it really means is that we should not cling to our past more than we should. In life, we continue climbing the rungs of the ladder of success but since we tend to think we have reached our zenith, we never continue moving upward. This is when the downward fall begins.

Understanding the concept of assets

What are assets? Assets are what you utilize in order to start empowering yourself financially. These assets include monetary as well as monetary resources. Most people only consider monetary assets when they speak about assets. They consider things like their bank balance, their property, their cars, their stocks, etc. as assets. However, there is much more to assets than just these materialistic things.

Here we take a look at assets other than the usual material ones.

Goodwill

Your good name in the market is a veritable asset. It could be your name or the name of your company, your brand, etc. Whatever goodwill your name has accumulated, you could certainly use it in improving your profits, and hence it becomes an asset. For instance, if you launch a new product with the same name of your previous successful product, it already gets a lot of foundation to succeed. That's the reason big name companies sell their goodwill when they give out franchises.

Your qualifications, eligibilities and experiences

Everything that you do in your life is an asset in itself. These are things you can tap into in order to empower yourself in a better manner. For example, if you are a postgraduate, you could use that qualification to pitch in for financing a research plant you want to set up. If you have worked in a particular area, your chances of earning in that area are more.

Your family, friends and other people

Everyone that you come in contact with is a potential asset for you. You are what your family makes you, and that decides your capabilities to a large extent. Also, your friends make you and so do other people that you come in contact with. People are so important to businesses today that there are complete business models that are set up on this concept. Take network marketing, for instance, better known as MLM, where people directly tap into the people they know in order to enhance their income capabilities.

Building your assets

Asset building is your first active step toward financial empowerment. You may have done various things in this journey, but it is in asset building that your journey really gains momentum. Being financially empowered means you have to have enough money so that you don't lack for funds when you need them. You have to be rich enough to have money to cover all your needs and desires. The desires part needs to be seen with more careful attention here, because most people have adequate money to cover their needs. It is when they need to realize one of their dreams that they feel they are lacking in proper funds.

It is necessary that you have the right kind of financial empowerment to chase your goals and intentions. This is where asset building becomes important in your route to financial empowerment. In this context, you try to build on what you can call your own so that you can build more to call your own. There are various ways in which you can begin focusing on asset building.

Proper investments

Investing is the best route to building assets. Find ways to make investments, such as in fixed deposits in banks, money-back insurance policies, stocks or whatever suits your interests. The channel you select for investment should be safe and should guarantee you high returns.

Sniffing out opportunities

Opportunities are all around us, but we don't know how to get at them. Keep your eyes wide open. If there is a business venture that interests you, learn more about it till you know all that there is to it. There are several high-paying opportunities like network marketing that can pay you back a lot without requiring much investment. Keep your mind receptive to such opportunities.

Involve your friends and family

Most of us shut out our near and dear ones when it comes to asset building. We have to understand that assets are not just monetary. There are various other things that can help us build ourselves financially, and toward this end, we have to realize that the role of the people in our lives is quite significant.

Investing in education for your financial empowerment

The journey has begun sooner than you think, but it hasn't ended yet. What we don't really realize is that our tryst with financial empowerment begins much sooner than we think.

It isn't when we are 20 and thinking about a career; it is right when we are 3 and attend our first school. In fact, our financial empowerment begins even before that when our parents lovingly and patiently tell us what is what. All those questions, all those attempts at gathering information and, later, education, are nothing but steps toward financially empowering ourselves.

For, what is education if not a way to empower ourselves in every way, including financially? A lot of people tap into their educational qualifications when they are looking for a job, pitching for a promotion, applying for a freelancing assignment or even when applying for financial assistance for a commercial venture. The educational qualification is a kind of abstract collateral; it is something people judge your financial worth with. If you are better qualified they know that you will keep sailing through and hence they don't mind extending a better financial help for your ventures. They don't mind investing in your ventures either because they consider you as a worthy candidate with their money.

That is the reason, it is important to learn as much as possible. After becoming the President of the United States, one of the first things Barack Obama did was to give a clarion call to his people to "go back to school". This does not really mean physically going back to school, but it means continuing to learn something or the other as we did when we were younger.

Come to think of it, when we were at school, we would learn a new thing each day. Are we doing that right now? At school, we enriched our minds each day and became what we are today. But why has this process of "becoming" stopped for some people? Why do some people think that their learning age has ceased? We need to educate ourselves continuously, till the last day of our lives and keep improving ourselves.

When we are more educated, we not only learn better avenues to earn money but we also learn how to manage the money properly so that it keeps growing. No form of education should be intimidating and there is no age when you cannot begin learning something.

Enriching your financial coffers with recreation

How does recreation help in building your financial value? Isn't this like shattering a myth? The common mentality of most people is that when they are getting some recreation for themselves – in whatever form that might be – they are actually wasting time. They think that by giving themselves some amusement, they are actually depriving themselves of the opportunity of being able to earn something. Proverbs like "Wasting time is akin to wasting money" don't help matters one bit. But we should remember that "All work and no play make Jack a dull boy." But, is it only a dull boy that Jack can turn out to be? No, worse things can happen if you deprive yourself from proper routes of recreation.

You have to understand what recreation means first. To recreate means to free up your mind and utilize it in doing something that you really like to do. It means to unwind yourself from your daily rigmarole of work. Since our mind is not a machine, but a living organ with blood and tissues in it, it does need this kind of unwinding ourselves.

But there is a subtle point that you must understand. Every person chooses his or her form of recreation and this is most times connected with what they do professionally. For example, for a person who teaches, reading could be a form of recreation. Now, this is actually helping their profession in various ways. This person is able to expand his or her knowledge and that really helps them in their profession. For a professional sportsperson, looking at someone else's game could be recreation. Now, they could pick up various tips from that and learn.

However, even when you think there are no obvious benefits of your form of recreation on your profession, there are actually several benefits. Consider that you have a desk job. Your mode of recreation is to shoot villains in computer games. How does this help your profession? It actually does, in a very poignant way, because it helps clear the clutter of monotony that your job has created and gives you a chance to do something that revitalizes your energy. You are refreshed and can even return to work the next day in a better mood.

Remember that empowering yourself financially does not mean immersing yourself in money-related thoughts and keeping yourself there all the time. Sometimes, you have to come out of those shackles and think in a liberated manner. This helps you rethink things and you begin looking at the world with a renewed perspective.

The long haul

Financially empowering yourself for the future – Yes, it's possible, but only if you act right now. It may not sound pleasant to a lot of us, but when most of us think of the term "financial empowerment", they tend to think about short-term goals. They think about how they can put in efforts to achieve money in the short term, within just a few weeks probably. One of the biggest mistakes that we do is that we contract our entire lifespan into a few weeks by thinking in this manner. We forget that we have a long life ahead of us and that if you want to be really financially empowered, we have to make sure that we have enough for that period which looms ahead of us.

That is why, when we speak about financial empowerment, it is not going to be much about what you can do that can give you returns today – there is a lot of material on that already – but it is about what you can do so that you stay financially empowered for the longer term. This is actually what must interest each and every one of us. There are some very important ways in which this can be done.

Education

Now, everyone gets basic education and hence if you want to really financially empower yourself, you have to learn something more than the other person. We aren't talking about childhood education here but education that enriches you as a professional. In the Internet marketing milieu, for example, a person who has educated himself or herself to use blogs and article submissions will do better than someone who uses just article submissions.

Investing

People who are in for the long haul will always think closely about investment options. They will think where they can invest so that they can get the best returns. Investment is highly important if you want to financially empower yourself because this is what can help you when the chips are down.

Insurance

Insurance is an assurance that is of value when something goes horribly wrong. There are several unforeseen things that can happen in our lives; one such stroke can wipe out all the financial empowerment that we have achieved for ourselves. Though any loss in the world can never be replenished completely, insurances do provide some respite in such events.

Recreation

Every song you hear, every book your read, every movie you watch, every place you visit enriches your mind in some way. Though you aren't doing these things for gaining knowledge, they are certainly expanding what you know. You are learning new things and anything can be important at any time. Hence, even the way you amuse your mind is essential when you are talking about financial empowerment.

All these things won't bring money right away at your doorstep, but they are definitely enhancing your capabilities. You become a better person, financially and otherwise, when you use these key factors in the right way.

Staying upwardly mobile

How do we ensure that we keep empowering ourselves financially? Our finishing touch will be to speak about how you must remain always moving toward the top. In fact, we have alluded to this already when we spoke about the Sum of Five. When you try to equate yourself with your collaborators and then find better collaborators if you find they are all doing much worse than you, you are staying upwardly mobile. When you mix around with people who have a particular kind of status, it automatically begins rubbing on you. Consciously or subconsciously, you begin taking steps to be with them, and sooner than you think, you are there. You get that one important breakthrough and you get to be with these people.

If you have used the four fundamentals in the right way, and are still constantly using them, then you will keep shaping yourself to be a more significant person financially. You will be going upward all the time and this is what really matters. One thing that you have to keep in mind is that you must broaden your approaches. Once you are set with something, move on to other things. We have spoken about how you must be always aware of opportunities and take them in your stride. Learn how to make the most of them.

Think positive. Think big. When you do that, you usually do big. If you confine yourself to thinking narrow-mindedly, you are going to stay there. A lot of modern philosophers have laid great emphasis on the importance of thought – Stephen Covey, Rhonda Byrne, Paulo Coelho – and you have to understand that there is great truth in this. When you think positively about something, things automatically energize themselves to make that happen. You know this fact in another form already probably – the Law of Attraction. Yes, this law can help you greatly in financially empowering yourself. Get acquainted with it today.

Conclusion

Financial empowerment is quite attainable, even if you have started with nothing. The fact is that most people don't think it can happen to them and hence they stay in the rut.

One of the most important things to materialize the things mentioned in this book is that you have to have the faith in yourself. Believe that you can make the transition. Believe that you can take that leap.

CHAPTER 10

WRAPPING IT UP

You made it to the end! I hope this book was an enlightening tool for you. Hopefully you took away some very key concepts to help you in your current business or help you get started in your very first business. Over many years in marketing, I have been very fortunate to learn, grow and profit in this business. There is no reason why you can't find the same success that I've had.

Apply the "hustle" and marketing instincts that will allow you to profit in your business. Remember, there are three components to your success: (1) continuous education, (2) sell, sell, sell and (3) take care of your leads and customers! Find the right opportunity at the right time, get with the right people and you will find that success is abound.

Now, there is one last thing for you to consider. This component has been one of the biggest keys to my success. Having a coach, mentor, business partner or just a friend to bounce ideas off of is vital to the success of your business.

No successful entrepreneur or successful company has been built without the help of a trusted advisor, business partner, mentor or just a friend. This is important for one very simple reason. Just because you think something is a good idea doesn't mean that it is. I can recall many times when I thought I had a good idea for a new product or marketing strategy but my mentor would eventually say, "That won't work." Very irritating at times but it's good to have someone that has been there, done that in your corner. This keeps us accountable as business owners and prevents us from making very costly mistakes.

So I challenge you to put all these resources to good use and apply them in your marketing. Business loves speed and so does money. This is why you have to get off your butt and stop talking about making money and take action. If you do not like your current outcome in life than it is time to change those outcomes with a new course of action. If you implement the information from this book, work hard, remain dedicated to your business, and face challenges head on with action than you to will be well on your way into successful entrepreneurship.

Stay In Touch and Join Our Team

If you would like to explore more "free" online marketing training than visit our website at http://jumpstartmarketing-concepts.com. We offer tons of training at no cost that will help you along the way in your online marketing journey. You can also link up with us on email at info@jsmarketingconcepts.com or any of our social media websites to include Facebook, Twitter, Pinterest, LinkedIn, YouTube, and Google +.

If you are interested in working with me direct for advice and mentorship you can set up a free strategy session any time at http://workwithjasonmiller.com

Thank you for taking the time out of your busy schedule to educate yourself. Education is important to your business success! Now go Forth and Conquer!

Our websites:

Main Corporate site: http://jumpstartmarketingconcepts.com

Patriot Team: http://patriotstobusiness.com

Patriot Community Outreach Program:
   http://patriotsoutreach.com

Jason T. Miller

Secret Solo Ad Training: http://mysolosecret.com
Work With Me Direct: http://workwithjasonmiller.com
Join Our Patriot Team: http://patriotsignup.com

PATRIOT COMMUNITY OUTREACH PROGRAM

Help someone that you know in need. This special card, when presented at most prescription counters, will save you up to 79% on the purchase of most prescription drugs. There is no obligation, no activation required and there are no fees to use this powerful card - just savings for the user!

In today's world of high prescription drug costs every little bit counts!

To learn more about this card, read testimonials of actual card users, download additional cards for your family and friends, and look up store locations and savings, visit our website at http://patriotsoutreach.com (This savings program is only available in the U.S.)

HELP US HELP MILLIONS OF PEOPLE TODAY!

PRINT A CARD OR GIVE ONE TO SOMEONE WHO NEEDS ONE TODAY! HELP US SAVE MILLIONS OF $$ TODAY!

http://patriotsoutreach.com

WHAT DO A FEW OF MY STUDENTS HAVE TO SAY?

"I love that Jason is honest about business! It takes determination and patience. Jason's coaching style is down-to-earth and easy to understand to lay people. Those that are new to business will be able to implement the scenarios discussed with ease! I sent him an email not quite understanding a few things and Jason took it upon himself to call me. After our call I was able to relax and understand the process better. I really appreciate Jason for reaching out to me the way he did. I'm lucky to have such an awesome coach! I felt confident that I could effectively apply the strategies my coach taught me. Jason Miller is wonderful!"

7-Figure Coaching Student

"Jason Miller has been a pleasure to work with. Once I found out we had military background we hit it off. Jason has been great explaining everything from the beginning. We have worked together to where I have my autoresponder set up completely and I'm ready to start building my email list for my business. He has been great with checking over my work to make sure I'm doing it right and when I'm not he explains in detail of what I need to change and why. Awesome Coach! What is great is I can always send a text through Skype and he always gets back to me quickly. It's nice to know he is just a click away.

What I like about Jason is I feel we will be friends even after our coaching lessons are over with. He is just that type of a person that makes you feel like a friend. He doesn't overpower you with information and makes sure you're comfortable with what you need to be doing. He makes you feel comfortable to talk to and ask those dumb questions. All I can say is I am thankful to have Jason Miller as my coach. Perfect fit!"

7-Figure Coaching Student

"Jason gets right to business AND is a great listener AND effectively moves the iceberg (me) in the right direction. It's great to know that I'm getting MAXIMUM value from every minute during my coaching sessions. Also, Jason's "no hype" approach to coaching is refreshing and effective. His ability to communicate with laser focus helps expand my vision AND confidence about my Internet business. This comes in handy when I'm spinning my wheels from information overload. Jason's mastery of skills necessary to be a coach are GREATLY APPRICIATED! Looking forward to all future sessions!"

7-Figure Coaching Student

"I have had 2 sessions with Jason Miller, plus I've gone through his training on YouTube. He is EXCELLENT. Jason is very easy to understand and very encouraging during our sessions. I was very impressed with Jason's dedication to his trainees as he was even doing coaching sessions with them on Skype while on vacation. Now that is DEDICATION!

His willingness to talk to us on our level and coach us through our questions and problems is amazing. We are looking forward to continuing our training with him when we arrive home from our trip. Jason doesn't hold anything back when he is teaching us and we really appreciate his openness. He is an Amazing Asset to have on your side in business and definitely to me"

7-Figure Coaching Student

"Jason may have been the absolutely perfect coach selection for me. I like his instruction methods and his ability to reduce the complex to the understandable. His willingness to happily spend more than the allocated time is much appreciated by me.

Friendly, punctual, knowledgeable, disciplined in staying on topic till I fully understood the subject. Always willing to critique and advise on copy. Provided answers to questions outside of the allotted and required time allocation. All in all a true professional who tells it like it is.

With still many more sessions available to me with Jason I would have to say I am deeply impressed with the caliber and integrity of his coaching. I'm happy that Jason is my coach. I believe it's a good fit."

7-Figure Coaching Student

"I love Jason. He is clear and well spoken. He understands my level and talks to where I am at in my business. He is patient with me and answers all my questions. He works well with my learning pace and me. He often spends more than the allotted with me on the Skype. He is thorough and keeps us on the subject matter. He is understanding of where I am at and able to move at my pace. Very open and willing to help me improve. Jason is a strong individual with good skills and good with people. I am very pleased with him and glad he is my coach."

7-Figure Coaching Student

www.ingramcontent.com/pod-product-compliance
Lightning Source LLC
Chambersburg PA
CBHW022110210326
41521CB00028B/182